TOP GRAMMAR

For Intermediate Students

중급 - 1

WorldCom

1. Forms

문법을 제대로 습득하기 위해서는 일정한 뜻을 나타내는 형식을 정확히 익혀야만 합니다. 특히 정확한 형태 습득은 문법 학습의 초기와 완성 단계에서 중요하기 때문에, 각 unit의 핵심적인 형태를 예문과 함께 제시했습니다. 예습과 복습용으로 활용합시다.

2. Meaning & Use

일정한 문법 형태가 어떤 뜻으로 어떻게 쓰이는지를 친절하게 설명했습니다. 단순한 암기가 아니라 이해를 통해 문법을 제대로 익힐 수 있도록 했습니다.

3. Key point

학교 내신시험, TOEIC Bridge, TOEIC, TEPS 등 주요 영어시험에 자주 출제되는 사항을 쉽게 이해할 수 있도록 설명했습니다. 꼼꼼히 익혀서 특목고 진학 등의 꿈을 이루는 바탕을 마련합시다.

4. Exercises

학교 내신시험이나 TOEIC 등 다양한 시험에 충분히 대비할 수 있도록 정밀하게 문제를 구성했습니다. 또한 문제 풀이를 통해 자연스러운 문법을 구사할 수 있도록 배려했으니 한 문제, 한 문제를 철저하게 익힙시다.

5. Chapter Review

각 chapter에서 학습한 사항을 완전히 자신의 것으로 만들 수 있도록 보다 다양한 유형과 활용도가 높은 예문으로 문제를 구성했습니다. 자신의 문법 실력을 한 차원 높이는 계기로 활용합시다.

이와 같은 과정을 통해 자연스럽고 정확한 영어를 구사할 수 있게 될 뿐만 아니라, TEPS 등 주요 영어시험에 완벽하게 대비할 수 있습니다. 차분히 과정을 밟아나갑시다.

수많은 영문법 교재가 출간되었음에도 불구하고 학생들의 문법 실력을 체계적이고 효율적으로 길러 주는 책을 찾기가 몹시도 어려운 실정입니다. 활용도가 현저히 떨어지는 사항을 자세하게 다루어 불필요하게 부담을 가중시키거나 다양한 영어 시험에 대비해야 하는 우리 학생들의 실정에 걸맞지 않는 사항에 치중하는 교재들이 흔합니다. 또한 학생들이 제대로 된 영어 실력을 갖출 수 있게 배려한 영문법 교재도 찾아보기 어렵습니다.

'Top Grammar'는 이와 같은 현실을 개선하기 위한 오랜 노력의 결과로 탄생한 문법 교재입니다. "조동사 used to의 부정형"과 같이 문법학자나 관심을 가질 만한 불필요한 사항은 과감히 배제하고 꼭 필요한 문법 사항을 체계적으로 이해할 수 있도록 배려했습니다. 또한 활용도가 높고 흥미로운 예문을 선택함으로써 본 교재의 학습을 통해 자연스럽게 영어 실력을 향상시킬 수 있도록 했습니다. 마지막으로 학교 내신시험 등 영문법 지식이 활용되는 모든 시험들에서 빈번하게 출제되는 사항을 깔끔하게 정리했습니다.

문법이란 뜻을 자연스럽게 구성하기 위한 약속입니다. 따라서 뜻과 모양, 그리고 쓰임새 사이의 유기적인 관계를 체계적으로 이해해야만 제대로 된 문법 실력, 더 나아가서, 영어 실력을 기를 수 있습니다. 이와 같은 점을 감안한 Top Grammar는 정말로 꼭 필요한 내용을 단기간내에 효율적으로 학습할 수 있도록 하나하나의 설명과 하나하나의 예문을 세심하게 배려한 최고의 문법서입니다. Top Grammar의 체계적인 문법 프로그램을 통해 진정한 문법 실력과 영어 실력을 기를 수 있게 되기를 간절히 기원합니다.

Practical English

모든 영문법 사항들이 일상적으로 빈번하게 쓰이지는 않는다. 원어민마저도 평생에 한 번도 쓰지 않는 문법 사항들도 많이 있다. TOP GRAMMAR는 일상적으로 빈번하게 쓰이는 실용적인 문법 사항들을 체계적으로 편성했다.

Living Grammar

자연스럽게 쓰이는 문장을 통해서야 비로소 문법은 생명력을 얻는다. 실제 용례(usage)가 뒷받침이 되지 않으면 문법은 생명을 잃고 만다. 이와 같은 점을 고려하여 TOP GRAMMAR는 원어민들이 자연스럽게 구사하는 예문을 중심으로 편성했다. 이처럼 "살아 있는 문법"을 학습해야만 탄탄한 문법 실력을 배양할 수 있을 뿐만 아니라 자연스러운 영어 구사력을 기를 수 있기 때문이다. TOP GRAMMAR의 생명력이 강한 예문을 통해 영어다운 영어를 구사할 수 있도록 하자.

Useful Language

학교 내신시험, 수능, TOEIC Bridge, TOEIC, TEPS 등 주요 영어시험에서는 여전히 문법의 비중이 상당하다. 이들 시험에서는 활용도가 높은 문법 사항들이 주로 출제되는데, TOP GRAMMAR는 이와 같은 빈출 사항들을 짜임새 있게 정리했다. 또한 TOEFL iBT의 Speaking과 Writing 영역에 활용될 수 있는 주요 사항들도 본문에서 다루었기 때문에, TOP GRAMMAR로 각종 영어시험의 문법 영역에 완벽히 대비할 수 있다.

American English

영국식 영어(British English)와 미국식 영어(American English)는 발음, 철자, 표현, 일부 문법 사항 등에서 다양한 차이를 나타낸다. 우리나라 학생의 경우는 초등학교부터 고등학교까지 미국식 영어로 학습을 하기 때문에 미국식 영어를 정확히 익히는 것이 올바른 순서이다. 학교 내신시험이나 수능 시험, 그리고 TOEFL iBT나 TEPS는 철저하게 미국식 영어를 측정한다. 반면 TOEIC의 경우는 발음에서만 일정 정도 영국식 영어를 채택했지만 독해나 문법은 완전히 미국식 영어를 측정한다. 따라서 우리나라 학생들은 무엇보다도 미국식 영어를 제대로 습득하는 것이 우선 순위이다. 이와 같은 점을 고려하여 TOP GRAMMAR는 철저하게 미국식 영어를 채택했다.

Engaging Learning Activities

문법 실력은 현실감 있는 상황에서 실제로 자연스러운 문법을 구사하는 연습을 통해서만 제대로 길러질 수 있다. 따라서 문법 문제 하나하나가 일상적인 상황에서 활용될 수 있는 능력을 측정하거나 학생의 흥미를 끌 수 있는 활동으로 구성되어야 한다. TOP GRAMMAR는 자연스러우면서도 흥미로운 예문과 다양한 문제 유형을 통해 학생들이 보다 쉽고 편안하게 문법에 다가갈 수 있도록 자상하게 배려했다. 또한 자연스러운 맥락에서 활용될 수 있는 문장들을 예문으로 선택함으로써 학생들이 일정한 문법 형태가 실제로 쓰이는 맥락(context)을 이해할 수 있게 했다. 따라서 TOP GRAMMAR를 학습함으로써 진정한 영어 실력을 흥미롭게 또한 체계적으로 기를 수 있다.

Contents

Chapter 1

동사의 종류

Form

1. The dark clouds **disappeared** and the rain **stopped**.
   I **met** her yesterday at the mall.

2. She **wept** for hours when her goldfish **died**.

3. I **forgot my wife's birthday**.

4. Melissa **entered** the room quietly.

5. We **waited for** her.

Meaning & Use

1_ 행위의 대상이 되는 목적어를 반드시 필요로 하는 동사를 타동사라고 하고 목적어가 필요 없는 동사를 자동사라고 한다.

We went to Thailand last year.

I blew the trumpet loudly.

2_ 자동사는 다른 대상을 필요로 하지 않는 행위를 나타내기 때문에 목적어가 오지 않는다. 그렇지만 부사나 전치사구는 올 수 있다.

Rain fell throughout the day.

3_ 타동사는 다른 대상을 필요로 하는 행위를 나타내기 때문에 목적어가 와야 한다.

My grandmother plants tomatoes as a hobby.

4_ 우리말로는 자동사처럼 느껴지지만 영어에서는 타동사인 경우가 종종 있다. 대표적인 예로 enter ~ (~에 들어가다), reach ~ (~에 도착하다), marry ~ (~와 결혼하다)를 들 수 있다.

Jenny married a famous doctor. (O) / Jenny married with a famous doctor. (X)

Tom reached Seoul yesterday. (O) / Tom reached to Seoul yesterday. (X)

5_ 우리말로는 타동사처럼 느껴지지만 영어에서는 자동사인 경우도 종종 있다. 대표적인 예로 wait for~ (~를 기다리다), complain of ~ (불평하다)를 들 수 있다.

Michelle complained of the noise. (O) / Michelle complained the noise. (X)

Exercises

A 적절한 것을 괄호 안에서 고르시오.

1 If you have any questions, (rise, raise) your hand.

2 The sun always (rises, raises) in the east.

3 The giant (fell, felled) the tree with a large axe.

4 Snakes (fell, felled) from the sky.

5 The woman (lay, laid) her baby on the sofa.

6 The poor old man (lay, laid) in his bed.

7 Many fans (waited, awaited) for the star to appear.

B 밑줄 친 부분이 어법에 맞으면 T, 맞지 않으면 F라고 쓰고 맞게 고치시오.

1 We played football game until sunset.   (   ) _____

2 Sarah went Toronto last month.   (   ) _____

3 Harold married with a nurse.   (   ) _____

4 Finally, we reached to the temple.   (   ) _____

5 Now, enter the entrance in an orderly fashion. (   ) _____

6 Time and tide wait no man.   (   ) _____

7 Sue complained a sharp pain.   (   ) _____

C 다음 글의 밑줄 친 부분 중, 어법상 틀린 것은?

A true friend is there for you all the time. A casual friend ①leaves you when you ②have a problem. A true friend feels happy when good things happen to you. A casual friend feels happy when bad things happen to you. A true friend cries with you when you are sad. A casual friend ③laughs you when you are sad. A true friend cheers you up when you ④fail. A casual friend does not care when you fail. A true friend never leaves you no matter what. A casual friend is not there for you when you ⑤need help.

Form

1 The food on the dinner table **smells** delicious.
He **runs** three miles every day to stay healthy.

2 I can't **stand it** when he **snores**.

3 If you add too much salt to the chicken, it won't taste **good**.

Meaning & Use

1_ 주어나 목적어의 상태를 설명하는 보어를 필요로 하는 동사를 불완전동사라고 하고, 보어가 필요 없는 동사를 완전동사라고 한다.

Mary became a famous scientist.

We returned from the woods.

2_ 완전동사는 크게 완전자동사와 완전타동사로 나눌 수 있다. 완전자동사는 목적어가 필요 없는 데 반해, 완전타동사는 목적어가 꼭 있어야 한다.

We worked for over twenty hours today.

I typed my essay on the computer.

3_ 불완전동사는 크게 불완전자동사와 불완전타동사로 나눌 수 있다. 불완전자동사는 목적어가 필요 없는 데 반해, 불완전타동사는 목적어가 반드시 있어야 한다. 불완전타동사가 쓰인 문장에서 보어는 목적어의 상태를 설명한다. 중요한 불완전자동사는 다음과 같다.

> appear be become feel get go look remain seem smell taste turn

After we heard the news, we felt much better.

The festival made all of us happy.

Key point _ 불완전자동사의 보어

불완전자동사의 보어로 명사나 형용사는 올 수 있지만 부사는 결코 올 수 없다. 부사는 본래 동사나 형용사를 꾸며주는 일을 하기 때문이다. 반면 형용사는 본래 명사가 나타내는 대상을 설명하기 때문에 보어로 쓰일 수 있다.

The milk tasted sour. (O) / The milk tasted sourly. (X)

The baby's skin felt soft. (O) / The baby's skin felt softly. (X)

Exercises

A   적절한 것을 괄호 안에서 고르시오.

1   Belle, you look (beautiful, beautifully) today!

2   To our great surprise, Jessica turned (a traitor, traitor).

3   When I met her boyfriend, I felt (terrible, terribly).

4   The strawberry ice cream tasted (greatly, great).

5   Strangely enough, the suspect remained (silent, silently).

6   When I broke her necklace, she went (madly, mad).

7   To be frank with you, your story seemed (strange, strangely).

B   밑줄 친 부분이 어법에 맞으면 T, 맞지 않으면 F라고 쓰고 맞게 고치시오.

1   In fact, many students got <u>angrily</u> with
    the teacher.   ( ) _____

2   When she heard the news, Sarah
    appeared <u>calmly</u>   ( ) _____

3   Unfortunately, the gap became <u>wider</u>.   ( ) _____

4   The dish smells <u>freshly</u>.   ( ) _____

5   The milk turned <u>sour</u>.   ( ) _____

6   You look <u>sadly</u>. What happened?   ( ) _____

7   My lunch tasted <u>funny</u>.   ( ) _____

C   다음 글의 밑줄 친 부분 중, 어법상 틀린 것은?

Betsy ① is my best friend. She always laughs at my jokes. Her jokes
make me laugh, too. She never worries about anything. I wonder how she
can be so ② happy. Sometimes I get ③ madly at some of my friends. Then
Betsy and I call them names together. After that, I feel much, much
④ better. Sometimes some friends make me feel ⑤ bad. Then Betsy
wants to hit them. Of course, I stop her from hitting them. But I really
thank her so much. She is really a good friend of mine.

Form

1 Tim **gave me a frog**.
My father always **makes us a hamburger** on Saturdays.

2 Mom **gave** an expensive car **to** me.

3 Chris **bought** a golden watch **for** me.

4 May I **ask** a question **of** you?

Meaning & Use

1_ "누구에게 무엇을 (해)주다"라는 구문을 만들어내는 동사를 수여동사라고 한다. 이때 "누구"에 해당하는 말을 간접목적어라고 하고 "무엇"에 해당하는 말을 직접목적어라고 한다.
Britney sent me a rude letter.
Alice made them a beef steak.

2_ 수여동사가 들어 있는 문장은 전치사를 써서 전환할 수 있는데, 이때 써야 하는 전치사에 따라 to를 쓰는 동사, for를 쓰는 동사, of를 쓰는 동사로 나뉜다. 바로 어떤 것을 주는 경우에는 to를, 다른 동작이 있은 다음에 주는 경우에는 for를 쓴다. 다음은 to를 써야 하는 주요 동사들이다.

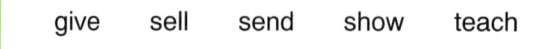

They sold me a big house. → They sold a big house to me.
Paris taught us French. → Paris taught French to us.

3_ 주기 전에 다른 동작이 있는 동사들은 문장 전환에서 for를 쓰는데, 다음이 주요 동사의 예이다.

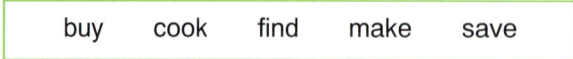

My father bought me a digital camera.
→ My father bought a digital camera for me.
Vivian saved us some cake. → Vivian saved some cake for us.

4_ 동사 ask의 경우에는 of를 써야 한다.
I'd like to ask you a favor. → I'd like to ask a favor of you.

Exercises

A 적절한 것을 괄호 안에서 고르시오.

1 Jenny cooked a cake (to, for) her old mother.

2 My homeroom teacher gave a boring book (to, of) me.

3 Barbara showed her house (to, for) her boyfriend.

4 Unfortunately, they couldn't find an office (to, for) the new reporter.

5 May I ask a favor (to, of) you?

6 My sister made a pretty doll (to, for) me.

7 Cindy taught Chinese (to, of) us.

B 밑줄 친 부분이 어법에 맞으면 T, 맞지 않으면 F라고 쓰고 맞게 고치시오.

1 Nancy gave a love letter <u>of</u> me. ( ) _____

2 My grandmother cooked a big meal <u>for</u> my father. ( ) _____

3 I want to ask a question <u>to</u> you. ( ) _____

4 The Smiths sold their house <u>of</u> a stranger. ( ) _____

5 My mom saved some lunch <u>for</u> me. ( ) _____

6 Anna found an apartment <u>of</u> us. ( ) _____

7 Sarah sent an early birthday gift <u>to</u> Billy. ( ) _____

C 다음 글의 밑줄 친 부분 중, 어법상 틀린 것은?

Once upon a time, there lived a kind fairy in Germany. Every day, she would ① help everyone. One day, an ugly old woman ② came to her and told her that she needed the fairy's blood to save her son. Without hesitation, the fairy gave her green blood ③ of the woman. After thanking the fairy, the old woman left. At that moment, the fairy felt ④ dizzy and fell down. When she opened her eyes, she knew that she was in heaven with God. The old woman happened to be God! He made a big palace ⑤ for her.

Form

1 I **expect** it to **rain** heavily tonight.
I **want** you **to take** me to the museum.

2 To our surprise, the principal **let** the students **have** a great party.
I **had** my picture **taken** at the mall yesterday.

3 I **heard** many voices **singing** in the distance.

Meaning & Use

1_ 목적어, 그리고 목적어의 상태나 동작을 설명하는 보어를 모두 필요로 하는 동사를 불완전타동사라고 한다. 불완전타동사로 구성되는 문장은 "목적어가 ~하는 것을 주어가 …하다"라는 뜻을 나타낸다. 불완전타동사의 보어로 to부정사가 오는 경우가 많은데, 중요한 예는 다음과 같다.

advise	allow	ask	expect	get	help	tell	want

The angry teacher didn't allow his students to go home.
Mary always helps me (to) do my homework. (help는 원형부정사가 올 수도 있음)

2_ "누가 ~하도록 시키다"라는 뜻을 나타내는 동사를 사역동사라고 하는데, 사역동사의 목적격보어로는 원형부정사 또는 과거분사(-ed)가 올 수 있다. 목적어가 일정한 동작을 할 때는 원형부정사가, 동작을 당할 때는 과거분사가 와야 한다. 중요한 사역동사는 다음과 같다.

let	make	have

We had the technician upgrade our computer.
We had our computer upgraded by the technician.

3_ "누가 ~하는 것을 관찰하다"라는 뜻을 나타내는 동사를 지각동사라고 하는데, 지각동사의 목적격보어로는 원형부정사나 현재분사, 그리고 과거분사(-ed)가 올 수 있다. 목적어가 일정한 동작을 할 때는 원형부정사나 현재분사를, 동작을 당할 때는 과거분사를 써야 한다. 중요한 지각동사는 다음과 같다.

feel	hear	see	watch

We saw him perform(ing) on stage.
I heard my name called in the middle of the night.

Exercises

A 적절한 것을 괄호 안에서 고르시오.

1 We need to have our car (fix, fixed) soon.

2 I want you (to lend, lent) me a few dollars.

3 We expected her (get, to get) there by five o'clock.

4 I felt the wind (blow, to blow) against my face.

5 Please, let me (to go, go). My daughter is waiting for me.

6 Marie had the thief (arrest, arrested) by the police.

7 The ugly teacher made his students (studied, study) really hard.

B 밑줄 친 부분이 어법에 맞으면 T, 맞지 않으면 F라고 쓰고 맞게 고치시오.

1 A littler girl asked me <u>called</u> you.　　　( ) _____

2 I heard the <u>singer</u> singing.　　　( ) _____

3 We saw the man <u>stolen</u> the DVD player.　　　( ) _____

4 Sue had her nails <u>doing</u> at the beauty shop.　　　( ) _____

5 All parents want their children <u>to be</u> happy.　　　( ) _____

6 His words made me <u>to feel</u> sick.　　　( ) _____

7 Finally, Jonathan let the bird <u>go</u>.　　　( ) _____

C 다음 글의 밑줄 친 부분 중, 어법상 틀린 것은?

When I was a kid, I was very ① <u>curious</u>. I wanted to know about everything. I was quite ② <u>interested</u> in watches. I always wondered what got them ③ <u>to work</u>. One day I decided to take apart my father's watch. I wanted to look at the inside of the watch. Finally, I took it apart. But I couldn't put it together. When my father came home and knew what happened, he got ④ <u>mad</u> at me and spanked me. But my curiosity paid off and made me ⑤ <u>to become</u> a great scientist.

Chapter Review

A   잘못된 곳을 고치시오.

1   My younger sister wept my wedding.

2   Susan married with a rich merchant.

3   A witch entered into the theater.

4   We need to discuss about the issue seriously.

5   The soldier complained a great pain in his leg.

6   Several hours later, they finally reached to the summit.

7   To our surprise, the loser looked happily.

8   Please, be quietly! I'm studying for an exam.

9   The pants felt really toughly.

10   In fact, I didn't get angrily at all.

11   Her wife seemed happily with the result.

12   To my disappointment, the juice turned sourly.

13   The woman sold the fake jewelry for a foolish man.

14   Eric bought an expensive apartment to his old mother.

15   Clara made a doghouse of her new puppy.

16   She saved a bowl of fruit to Michael.

17   I want to ask a big favor to you.

18   My English teacher gave a good grammar of me.

19   My nephew always sends a lovely letter of me.

20   I asked Sandra help me with my homework.

21   Jennifer had her ears to pierce with Sally.

22   We watched the night sky to darken as the sun went down.

23   I saw her expression to change from sad to happy.

24   Let me to go! I really want to go home.

25   Suddenly, I felt my heart to beat faster.

B (A), (B), (C)의 각 괄호 안에서 어법에 맞는 표현을 골라 짝지은 것으로 가장 적절한 것은?

Once upon a time, there lived a bad king in Czechoslovakia. One day, a handsome young man came to the king. The handsome young man wanted to (A) [marry / marry with] the king's pretty princess. But the king told the young man (B) [find / to find] him magic gold. With the help of three fairies, the handsome young man brought the gold to the king. When he touched the gold, the king turned into a frog. The princess felt (C) [sad / sadly] about this and killed the young man.

	(A)	(B)	(C)
①	marry	find	sadly
②	marry with	find	sad
③	marry	to find	sadly
④	marry with	to find	sadly
⑤	marry	to find	sad

C 다음 글의 밑줄 친 부분 중, 어법상 틀린 것은?

The Internet is very ① useful, but you should be careful about using it. For example, you've gotten a new e-mail account. Of course, you've gotten a password, too. Can you give the password ② to your best friend? No, of course not. In fact, he or she doesn't want you ③ to give them your password. You are chatting with somebody on the Internet. You hear her ④ to say that she is a pretty eleven-year-old girl. Can you believe that? In fact, she may expect you ⑤ to be a fool.

Chapter Review

D   다음 밑줄 친 부분에 가장 적절한 것을 고르시오.

1   Now _____ your chair, please.
   a. rise   b. raise
   c. to rise   d. raised

2   To our great surprise, the tall building _____ down in a second.
   a. felled   b. fells
   c. fallen   d. fell

3   The captain _____ a great pain in her chest.
   a. complained   b. complained of
   c. complaining of   d. complaining

4   Finally, the scientists _____ the desert island.
   a. reached to   b. reaching to
   c. reaches   d. reached

5   Kevin _____ an ugly princess.
   a. married to   b. married with
   c. married   d. married about

6   His story seemed too _____ to believe.
   a. strangely   b. strangeness
   c. strangers   d. strange

7   The handkerchief felt _____.
   a. softly   b. softness
   c. soft   d. softnesses

8   Many foreigners told me that kimchi tasted _____.
   a. deliciously   b. delicious
   c. deliciousness   d. more deliciously

9   Alice looked so _____ in her red dress.
   a. beautifully   b. beauty
   c. beauties   d. beautiful

10 When the students read the newspaper, they went _____.
   a. madly   b. mad
   c. madness   d. more madly

11 To my great surprise, the secretary sent a letter _____ me.
    a. of   b. from
    c. to   b. in

12 I want to ask a hard question _____ you.
    a. of   b. to
    c. at   b. by

13 His friend sold the old TV _____ him just for five dollars.
    a. of   b. to
    c. at   b. in

14 Mr. Carter taught Japanese _____ them.
    a. of   b. in
    c. at   b. to

15 The kind maid found a nice room _____ us.
    a. of   b. in
    c. for   d. to

16 We want you _____ the wonderfully made film.
    a. watch   b. watched
    c. to watch   d. watches

17 We have our milk _____ to us every morning.
    a. deliver   b. to deliver
    c. delivers   d. delivered

18 I saw the dog _____ on his hind legs.
    a. to stand   b. stand
    c. stands   d. to standing

19 The kind teacher advised me _____ to my heart.
    a. listen   b. listened
    c. listens   d. to listen

20 The boring movie made me _____ very often.
    a. to yawn   b. yawned
    c. yawn   d. yawns

Chapter 2

시제

Form

1 My parents **run** this shop.

2 I **eat** a late dinner every night.

3 Water **boils** at 100℃.

4 The next plane **leaves** at 3:30 in the afternoon.

5 If she **comes** home, tell her to call me.

Meaning & Use

1 _ 현재시제는 현재의 일반적인 상태나 동작을 나타낸다. 현재의 일시적인 상태나 감정도 현재
시제를 써서 표현함도 알아두어야 한다.

We live in Seoul.

Audrey lost the game and she is still angry about it.

2 _ 현재시제는 현재의 반복적인 습관을 나타낼 때도 쓰인다.

Sam teases his sister all the time.

3 _ 변하지 않는 과학적 사실은 언제나 현재시제로 표현된다.

Iron melts at 1538℃.

4 _ 시간표 등에 의해 확정된 미래의 일정은 현재시제로 표현된다.

School starts next month for most districts.

5 _ when이나 if가 이끄는 시간이나 조건의 부사절에서는 미래시제가 아니라 현재시제를
써야 한다.

When you come to South Korea, be sure to call me. (O)

When you will come to South Korea, be sure to call me. (X)

If you want to see me, contact my secretary. (O)

If you will want to see me, contact my secretary. (X)

Exercises

A 적절한 것을 괄호 안에서 고르시오.

1 Helium (boils, boiled) at -268.9℃.

2 School (is ending, ends) at noon on Fridays.

3 If I (marry, will marry) Ann, we will live happily.

4 When you (will travel, travel) to Toronto, you will see many tall buildings.

5 If I (miss, will miss) the train, I won't make it to the party.

6 When you (visit, will visit) the village, you will meet a strange guy.

7 If they (will find, find) this out, they will go mad.

B 밑줄 친 부분이 어법에 맞으면 T, 맞지 않으면 F라고 쓰고 맞게 고치시오.

1 We <u>live</u> in Mexico last year.   ( ) _____

2 Ozone <u>is</u> made up of three oxygen atoms. ( ) _____

3 The Han River <u>is</u> located in Korea.   ( ) _____

4 If we <u>will leave</u> right away, we won't be late. ( ) _____

5 When she <u>came</u> home, we will welcome her. ( ) _____

6 If you <u>will know</u> the answer, let me know. ( ) _____

7 When the train <u>leaves</u>, everyone will applaud. ( ) _____

C 다음 글의 밑줄 친 부분 중, 어법상 틀린 것은?

Did you know that too much noise can make you ① sick? Yes, it can. This is called "noise pollution." Some people ② think that noise is not a problem at all. But if you ③ will be surrounded by too much noise, you will lose your hearing. Too much noise can also give a lot of stress ④ to you. You see, stress ⑤ is the number one cause of a lot of diseases. So, you need to get away from noise.

과거시제

Form

> 1 We **saw** an amazing play at the theater last week.
>
> 2 I often **woke** up very early in the morning.
>   I **would** wake up very early in the morning.
>
> 3 There **used to be** a large building in my neighborhood.
>
> 4 My tutor told me that World War I **broke** out in 1914.

Meaning & Use

1_ 과거시제는 과거에 일어난 일을 나타낼 때 쓰인다. 동사의 과거형은 대개 -ed를 넣어 만들지만 see처럼 불규칙한 과거형을 쓰는 동사들도 있다. 중요한 예는 다음과 같다.

[불규칙 동사표는 부록 참조]

beat — beat	burst — burst	cost — cost
dig — dug	freeze — froze	hang — hung [hanged: 교수형에 처했다]
lay — laid	lie — lay	mistake — mistook
ride — rode	see — saw	wake — woke

The lake froze again last night.

2_ 과거의 습관은 과거시제로 표현할 수 있다. 또한 "would＋동사원형"이나 "used to＋동사원형"을 써서 나타낼 수도 있다.

The boys often played in the sandbox in the school playground.

The boys used to play in the sandbox in the school playground.

3_ "used to＋동사원형"은 현재와 다른 과거의 상태를 나타낼 수도 있다. 반면 "would＋동사원형"에는 이런 쓰임새가 없다.

Janine used to be rich, but she is very poor now.

4_ 역사적 사실은 과거시제로 표현한다. 역사적 사실이 다른 문장의 일부가 되어도 시제의 변화 없이 과거 시제를 써야 한다.

My history teacher told me that the Civil War broke out in 1861. (O)

My history teacher told me that the Civil War had broken out in 1861. (X)

Exercises

A 적절한 것을 괄호 안에서 고르시오.

1 My aunt would (visit, visited) us on Saturdays.

2 Sam (has spoken, spoke) to us at the meeting last night.

3 The book (costed, cost) me $500!

4 Clive was (hung, hanged) for trafficking illegal drugs.

5 Stella (lay, laid) her baby in the crib.

6 Daniel (used to, would) be a nice guy, but he is a jerk now.

7 The French navy (had invaded, invaded) Chosun in 1866.

B 밑줄 친 부분이 어법에 맞으면 T, 맞지 않으면 F라고 쓰고 맞게 고치시오.

1 They <u>beated</u> him black and blue last night. (   ) _____

2 Steve <u>hung</u> up his coat and entered the room. (   ) _____

3 Ruth <u>laid</u> on the sand for hours. (   ) _____

4 People often <u>mistaked</u> me for my brother. (   ) _____

5 Carole <u>used to</u> be a chef. (   ) _____

6 The French Revolution <u>has started</u> in 1789. (   ) _____

7 Columbus <u>discovered</u> America in 1492. (   ) _____

C 다음 글의 밑줄 친 부분 중, 어법상 틀린 것은?

I ① was born in a small village. The villagers believed that only good grades at school could make people happy, and my father was no exception. He always told us to study really hard. He did not allow us ② to draw pictures or sing songs. He ③ thought those activities were not good for school learning. One day my older sister ④ has taught me how to draw a picture. She was really good at drawing, and I admired her. But when my father saw what we were doing, he got mad and ⑤ hit my sister. Twenty years later, thanks to my sister, I became a great painter.

Form

1 Oil prices **will** increase in the long run.
It's cloudy. I think it's **going to** rain.

2 Your bag looks heavy. I**'ll** help you carry it.
We**'re going to** throw a surprise party for Deborah.

3 If you **attend** the film festival, you **will** be impressed.

Meaning & Use

1_ 미래시제는 미래에 대한 예측을 나타낼 수 있다. 일반적인 사실에 바탕을 두어 예측할 때는 will을, 현재 사실에 바탕을 두어 예측할 때는 be going to를 쓴다.

The Earth will become warmer.

We've just missed the bus. We're going to be late.

2_ 미래시제는 미래에 대한 계획을 나타낼 수 있다. 미리 계획을 세운 경우에는 be going to를 쓰는 데 반해, 바로 결정한 경우에는 will을 쓴다.

We're going to move to Seattle next year.

I'm busy at the moment. I'll talk to you about this later.

3_ 미래시제와 어울리는 if절에서는 현재시제나 현재완료형을 써야 함에 유의해야 한다.

If you finish the work in time, you will be given a vacation. (O)

If you will finish the work in time, you will be given a vacation. (X)

Key point_ **if절의 쓰임새**

학교 내신시험에서는 if절이 명사절인지 부사절인지를 구별할 것을 요구하는 문제를 자주 출제한다. if절이 "~인지"로 해석되는 명사절일 때는 if 다음에 미래시제가 올 수 있기 때문이다. 이런 경우 if 바로 앞에는 흔히 know, wonder 등의 동사가 온다.

I wonder if Michelle will win the race tomorrow. (O)

I wonder if Michelle wins the race tomorrow. (X)

Exercises

A   적절한 것을 괄호 안에서 고르시오.

1. What? Barbara is in the hospital? I (am going to, will) come and see her.
2. If you (visit, will visit) the museum, you will be amazed.
3. I wonder if it (rains, will rain) tomorrow.
4. We've just heard that Julie needs some help. We (are going to, will) help her.
5. We've already decided what to do with it. We (are going to, will) sell it.
6. I really want to know if Wendy (comes, will come) back home alive.
7. If you (don't, won't) want it, just throw it away.

B   밑줄 친 부분이 어법에 맞으면 T, 맞지 않으면 F라고 쓰고 맞게 고치시오.

1. The world's population <u>will</u> grow in the long run.   ( ) _____
2. Oh, he's injured! I <u>will</u> call the ambulance.   ( ) _____
3. If she <u>will see</u> her daughter, she will cry a lot.   ( ) _____
4. I wonder if Hillary <u>wins</u> the election next year.   ( ) _____
5. If he <u>won't attend</u> the event, it will disappoint me.   ( ) _____
6. We're <u>going to spend</u> some time in Paris next month.   ( ) _____
7. If you <u>want</u> more information, contact us.   ( ) _____

C   다음 글의 밑줄 친 부분 중, 어법상 틀린 것은?

Do you know that Samsung ① <u>is going to make</u> cellphones that spray perfume? It's true. When they ② <u>will get</u> a call, they will spray perfume. Do you think it is a good idea? Some people think so. They say that perfume makes your cellphone ③ <u>smell good</u>. It makes people like your cellphone and you. Others disagree. The perfume may make your clothes ④ <u>wet</u>. The cellphone may be larger. ⑤ <u>Will Samsung sell</u> such cellphones soon? Well, what do you think? Will they?

Unit 04 현재완료

Form

> 1 I **have** just **finished** writing the report.
>   Nancy **has** never **eaten** sushi before.
>
> 2 Harold **has gone** to Paris.
>   We **have lived** in Seoul for fifteen years.
>
> 3 They **have visited** the place many times.
>   They **visited** the place last year.
>
> 4 Susie **has done** many things since she **came** here.

Meaning & Use

1_ 현재완료는 과거에 일어난 일이 현재까지 영향을 미치고 있음을 나타낼 때 쓰인다. 「have [has]＋과거분사」라는 형태를 취하는데, 대개 함께 쓰이는 부사(구)에 따라 쓰임새가 달라진다. already, just, now, yet 등과 쓰일 때는 "~를 끝냈다"라는 완료의 용법으로, before, never, once 등과 쓰일 때는 "~한 적이 있다"는 경험의 용법으로 쓰인다.

They have already arrived there.

Sarah has once visited the White House.

2_ 현재완료는 과거에 일어난 일의 현재 결과를 나타낼 수도 있다. 그리고 since나 for와 함께 쓰여 "계속 ~하다"라는 뜻을 나타내기도 한다.

I have lost my watch. (＝And I haven't found it yet.)

We have dated for three years.

3_ 현재완료는 과거와 현재를 연결하는 것이기 때문에 분명하게 과거만을 나타내는 ago, yesterday, last year와 같은 표현과 함께 쓰일 수 없다. 이와 같은 표현들은 과거시제와 함께 쓰인다.

Elizabeth has visited her mother last week. (X)

Elizabeth visited her mother last week. (O)

4_ "~한 이래로"라는 뜻을 나타내는 since는 바로 다음에 과거시제를 써야 하며, 그 앞에는 현재완료를 써야 한다.

My eyes have gotten worse since I was a child.

Exercises

A 적절한 것을 괄호 안에서 고르시오.

1 Mary (has talked, talked) to the principal of the school yesterday.

2 Mr. Smith, a young woman (called, has called) you just now.

3 We (have walked, walked) through the entire woods last night.

4 I haven't (eaten, ate) anything yet.

5 Willow (loved, has loved) Xander since she was twelve.

7 I (have sent, sent) you a letter last week.

8 We (climbed, have climbed) the mountain ten years ago.

B 밑줄 친 부분이 어법에 맞으면 T, 맞지 않으면 F라고 쓰고 맞게 고치시오.

1 My child <u>has read</u> Harry Potter over four times. ( ) _____

2 Have you been to Europe <u>ago</u>? ( ) _____

3 There <u>were</u> many accidents since he became mayor. ( ) _____

4 He <u>has not taught</u> mathematics to children before. ( ) _____

5 We <u>have thrown</u> him a surprise party yesterday. ( ) _____

6 Ethan <u>hated</u> his brother since he was a teenager. ( ) _____

7 The years <u>have gone</u> by so quickly. ( ) _____

C 다음 글의 밑줄 친 부분 중, 어법상 틀린 것은?

① <u>Have you ever heard</u> of the All-American Girls' Professional Baseball League? As you can guess from the name, it was an American women's baseball league. The league was started in 1943 and ② <u>has ended</u> in 1954. Philip Wrigley helped start the league because he wanted baseball ③ <u>to continue</u>. Most American men fought in World War II, and there ④ <u>were</u> few men who could play baseball. Was the league a success? Yes, it ⑤ <u>was</u>, especially in the first few years. But later, its popularity declined. The league showed, however, that women can be excellent baseball players.

Form

1 Lisa **had taught** math for seven years before she quit.

2 Julie was thirty. She **had practiced** yoga for almost ten years.

3 We **will have reached** our destination by tonight.

Meaning & Use

1_ 과거완료는 과거의 일정한 시점보다 이전에 일어난 일을 나타낼 때 쓰인다. 「had + 과거분사」라는 형태를 취한다.

We had driven the car for more than ten thousand miles before we sold it.

She had finished all the assignments before the end of class.

2_ 과거완료는 또한 과거의 일정 시점까지 계속된 상황을 나타낼 수 있다.

Daniel was forty. He had taught German for almost twenty years.

3_ 미래완료는 「will have + 과거분사」라는 형태로 미래의 시점에 이루어질 일을 나타내는 데 쓰인다.

They will have finished the project a few days before the deadline.

Key point_ 미래완료의 쓰임새

TOEIC 등의 시험에서는 미래완료가 대개 미래의 일정한 때에 이르러 완료될 일을 나타낼 때 쓰인다는 점을 종종 출제한다. 흔히 by 또는 by the time과 어울린다는 점을 기억하고 미래완료의 형태를 정확히 익혀두어야 한다.

They will have eaten everything by the time their father returns. (O)

They had eaten everything by the time their father returns. (X)

Exercises

A 적절한 것을 괄호 안에서 고르시오.

1 She (has, had) learned to play the piano before she took violin lessons.
2 I (had, have) checked over it many times before you discovered the errors.
3 He (has, had) eaten the last peanut before we reached the grocery store.
4 She (had, has) fallen off his bike before we made it to the third hill.
5 Tara will (had, have) been married by then.
6 They will (have, had) given an explanation by the time the police leave.
7 There will (had, have) been many thunderstorms by the end of spring.

B 밑줄 친 부분이 어법에 맞으면 T, 맞지 않으면 F라고 쓰고 맞게 고치시오.

1 Drew <u>has put</u> gas in the car before we left. (   ) _____
2 Laura <u>had caused many</u> problems before she quit. (   ) _____
3 I <u>will have eaten</u> a few things before we had lunch. (   ) _____
4 She <u>had worked</u> there before she got a real job. (   ) _____
5 They <u>will had discovered</u> a cure by then. (   ) _____
6 You <u>will have learn</u> the language by then. (   ) _____
7 I <u>will have used</u> up all of the glue by tomorrow. (   ) _____

C 다음 글의 밑줄 친 부분 중, 어법상 틀린 것은?

Last night, my cellphone ① <u>saved</u> my life. I was at a crosswalk, about to cross the street. I ② <u>thought</u> the traffic lights turned green. So I started to walk. At that moment, my cellphone rang. I hesitated for a moment. Then I decided ③ <u>to take</u> the call, so I stopped walking. At that very moment, a small van just ④ <u>passed</u> by me. In fact, the car almost hit me. I was so surprised that I couldn't think at all. After a moment I realized that my cellphone ⑤ <u>will have saved</u> my life. My cellphone was really a lifesaver.

현재진행형·과거진행형

Form

1 We **are eating** pizza at the restaurant right now.

2 Amy **loves** her mother so much.
   Angela **resembles** her father.

3 The dog **was chasing** the cat around the yard.

4 Chris **was taking** a shower when the telephone rang.

Meaning & Use

1_ 현재진행형은 「am [are, is] + -ing」라는 형태를 취하며, 현재의 일반적인 상태나 동작이 아니라 현재의 일시적인 상태나 동작을 나타낸다.

Linda is talking on the phone with her grandparents right now.

The store is opening at this moment.

2_ 일시적인 상태나 동작을 나타내지 않기 때문에 진행형으로 쓸 수 없는 동사들이 있다.
중요한 예는 다음과 같다.

인지/감정:	know	understand	want	dislike	hate	like	love
외양:	appear	resemble	seem			
소유/존재:	belong	have	own	exist		

I want to have a car. (O) / I am wanting to have a car. (X)

Chris seems happy. (O) / Chris is seeming happy. (X)

In fact, UFOs do not exist. (O) / In fact, UFOs are not existing. (X)

3_ 과거진행형은 「was [were] + -ing」라는 형태를 취하며, 과거의 일반적인 상태나 동작이 아니라 과거의 일시적인 상태나 동작을 나타낸다.

We were watching a very scary movie.

4_ 과거에 하나의 동작이 계속되고 있는데 다른 동작이 이를 방해하는 경우에 방해하는 동작은 과거시제로, 방해 받는 동작은 과거진행형으로 나타낸다.

Oz was reading the newspaper when Melissa came in.

Exercises

A 적절한 것을 괄호 안에서 고르시오.

1 My father (reads, is reading) the newspaper right now.

2 Many students (are hating, hate) the strict teacher.

3 Cloe (resembles, is resembling) her grandmother.

4 The car (is belonging, belongs) to me.

5 In fact, they (own, are owning) many buildings in the city.

6 Jesicca (does not understand, is not understanding) Japanese.

7 As a matter of fact, aliens (are not existing, do not exist)

B 밑줄 친 부분이 어법에 맞으면 T, 맞지 않으면 F라고 쓰고 맞게 고치시오.

1 We <u>are watching</u> a football game on TV right now.　　　( ) _____

2 Many teenagers <u>are wanting</u> to be movie stars.　　　( ) _____

3 Every mother <u>loves</u> her children.　　　( ) _____

4 I <u>am having</u> five sisters.　　　( ) _____

5 The question <u>is seeming</u> difficult.　　　( ) _____

6 Some people <u>are disliking</u> animals.　　　( ) _____

7 We <u>were playing</u> video games when the phone rang.　　　( ) _____

C 다음 글의 밑줄 친 부분 중, 어법상 틀린 것은?

At the moment, I ① <u>am learning</u> English at school. I enjoy practicing English. I ② <u>am loving</u> the rhythm of this strange language. Because of this language, I ③ <u>understand</u> that language is anything but usual. Before I began to learn English, I ④ <u>had taken</u> language for granted. But the strangeness of the language made me ⑤ <u>realize</u> that language is very special. In addition, I have realized that language is more than a combination of words and phrases.

Chapter Review

A   잘못된 곳을 고치시오.

1   We go to the supermarket yesterday.

2   Mercury boiled at 357℃.

3   When you will finish writing the paper, let me know immediately.

4   If Michelle will come home, tell her to call me.

5   Bob has given me a gift yesterday.

6   The Spanish-American War has broken out in 1898.

7   Some people digged the grave.

8   Many turtles lied their eggs on the seashore.

9   What? She's injured? I am going to get there right away.

10   If you will fail the exam, your parents will be disappointed.

11   We want to know if you came to help us tomorrow.

12   If the world will end, we won't be able to enjoy the beauty of nature.

13   They have walked over ten kilometers yesterday.

14   She has never been to Europe ago.

15   I learned many useful things since I came here.

16   Jenny has finished writing her new book just now.

17   I have met the mayor of the city last weekend.

18   We will have never been outside of the country before we came here.

19   Almost all the students will have graduate by then.

20   I will have visit the library before I came to the meeting.

21   Scientists will had visited Mars by 2020.

22   I am knowing Alice quite well.

23   The fish are swim together in one big school.

24   Interestingly enough, the old castle is belonging to the beggar.

25   The king is having three beautiful daughters.

B (A), (B), (C)의 각 괄호 안에서 어법에 맞는 표현을 골라 짝지은 것으로 가장 적절한 것은?

Our annual school festival (A) [has been / was] held last week. It was great fun. I particularly enjoyed the song contest. My friend Sarah sang "One Summer Night" and won first prize. She sang it so beautifully that everyone there was deeply touched. I also liked the "dunk the teacher" tank. You see, when a student bought a basketball, she could throw it to dunk a teacher. It was great fun to see our teachers (B) [plunge / to plunge] into water. Some students suggested that we have a "kick the teacher" booth. But most students didn't like the idea. Anyway, I (C) [will not / has not] forget this year's school festival.

	(A)	(B)	(C)
①	has been	plunge	will not
②	was	to plunge	has not
③	has been	plunge	has not
④	was	plunge	has not
⑤	was	plunge	will not

C 다음 글의 밑줄 친 부분 중, 어법상 틀린 것은?

An electronic dictionary is a handy tool for learning languages. It is a very small device, but can do many things for you. Above all, it lets you ①look up words very easily. Just type a word you are looking for, and the gadget ②will find it for you. When you ③won't be sure about the spelling of a word, such a dictionary will help you by listing many words. Just look at the words, and you will find the very word you ④are looking for. An electronic dictionary can also pronounce words for you. So you can learn how to pronounce words corrctly. In these ways, electronic dictionaries help you ⑤learn languages very quickly.

Chapter Review

D   다음 밑줄 친 부분에 가장 적절한 것을 고르시오.

1   Lead _____ at 1,744℃.
    a. boiled   b. boils
    c. had boiled   d. was boiled

2   They _____ a small restaurant last year.
    a. run   b. have run
    c. ran   d. will have run

3   If you _____ really hard, you will be able to do anything.
    a. will try   b. tried
    c. had tried   d. try

4   When you _____ anything, give us a call, please.
    a. will remember   b. remembered
    c. remember   d. has remembered

5   My history teacher told us that Germany _____ reunified in 1990.
    a. has been   b. have been
    c. will have been   d. was

6   Because she was so angry, Xena suddenly _____ up the phone.
    a. hung   b. hanged
    c. hangs   d. hunged

7   The child _____ on the sand all day long.
    a. laid   b. lay
    c. lain   d. lays

8   Too many people _____ her for her cousin.
    a. mistaked   b. mistaken
    c. mistook   d. mistooked

9   We wonder if the new president _____ the economy soon.
    a. recovering   b. will recover
    c. recover   d. has recover

10   If you _____ Japan, you will meet many friendly people.
    a. will visit   b. visit
    c. visited   d. had visited

11 We know she's in the hospital. We _____ send her some flowers.

a. used to   b. have

c. are going to   d. had

12 When the winner _____ , everybody will applaud.

a. will come   b. comes

c. had come   d. used to come

13 Marie _____ many places in Europe since she was a child.

a. visited   b. used to visit

c. would visit   d. has visited

14 Have you ever _____ to the States before?

a. were   b. been

c. used to be   d. was

15 We have _____ finished our dinner.

a. just now   b. ago

c. yesterday   d. just

16 They have lived in the village _____ almost thirty years.

a. since   b. already

c. during   d. for

17 I _____ for more than ten hours before we left.

a. have slept   b. had slept

c. sleep   d. will have slept

18 They will _____ the problem by the time we get there.

a. had solved   b. have solve

c. has solve   d. have solved

19 We _____ that learning a foreign language is a difficult process.

a. understand   b. are understanding

c. were understanding   d. will be understanding

20 We _____ computer games when Mom entered our room.

a. are playing   b. were playing

c. will be playing   d. will have played

Chapter 3

태

Form

1 The last cookie **was eaten** by my little brother.
This cake **was made by** my grandmother.

2 English **is spoken** in Canada.

3 Some money **was stolen** from the office.

Meaning & Use

1_ 앞에서 살펴봤듯이, 타동사는 반드시 행위의 대상을 가진다. 행위의 주체를 주어로 하는 표현을 능동태(the active voice)라 하고, 행위의 대상을 주어로 하는 표현을 수동태(the passive voice)라 한다. 수동태는 「be 동사＋과거분사＋by ～」라는 형식을 취한다.

My little brother　ate　the last cookie. (능동태)

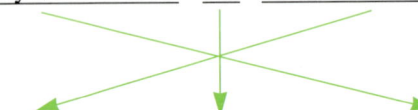

The last cookie　was eaten　by my little brother. (수동태)

2_ 이처럼 수동태는 행위의 대상에 중점을 두는 표현이기 때문에, 행위의 주체가 관심의 대상이 아니다. 따라서 행위의 주체가 분명한 경우에는 종종 생략된다.

The tape was rented from the local video shop.

3_ 또한 행위의 주체를 알 수 없는 경우에도 생략이 가능하다.

To our great surprise, the horse was killed.

Key point_ 수동태의 형태

TEPS 와 같은 어학능력시험에서는 수동태의 형태가『be 동사＋과거분사』라는 점을 종종 출제한다. 특히 be 동사 다음에 동사원형이 올 수 없음에 유의해야 한다. 일부 경우를 제외하고는 be 동사 다음에 동사 원형이 오는 경우는 없다.

The napkins on the table were blown away by the wind. (O)

The napkins on the table were blow away by the wind. (X)

Exercises

A 적절한 것을 괄호 안에서 고르시오.

1 The light was (turned, turn) on by my father.

2 The ring was (wear, worn) by many famous queens of Europe.

3 Unfortunately, all of our lakes were (polluted, pollute).

4 The television was (steal, stolen) by burglars last night.

5 Holly was (treated, treat) fairly at the company where she worked.

6 The chicken was (roast, roasted) in the oven.

7 My bike was (sold, sell) to the highest bidder at the auction.

B 밑줄 친 부분이 어법에 맞으면 T, 맞지 않으면 F라고 쓰고 맞게 고치시오.

1 Many guests were <u>invite</u> to the reception. ( ) _____

2 The Revolutionary War was <u>win</u> by the Americans. ( ) _____

3 The issue was <u>mentioned</u> in the newspaper article. ( ) _____

4 They were <u>followed</u> by the police. ( ) _____

5 Romeo was <u>treat</u> by a very famous doctor. ( ) _____

6 The letter was <u>wrote</u> in red ink. ( ) _____

7 The political party was <u>lead</u> by a scientist. ( ) _____

C 다음 글의 밑줄 친 부분 중, 어법상 틀린 것은?

In Type I questions, you first ① <u>read</u> a passage about academic topics. Then, you will listen to a lecture about the same topic. The lectures either support or ② <u>challenge</u> the passage. After that, you will be ③ <u>give</u> twenty minutes to compare the lecture with the passage. When actually ④ <u>writing</u>, you can read the passage again. You cannot, however, ⑤ <u>listen</u> to lecture again.

Form

> 1 I **was given a picture book** for my birthday.
>   A picture book **was given to me** for my birthday.
>
> 2 These cookies **were cooked for me** by my mother.
>
> 3 She **was asked** some difficult questions.

Meaning & Use

1_ 수여동사가 구성하는 문장을 4형식 문형이라고 하는데, 수여동사가 두 개의 목적어를 갖기 때문에 두 개의 수동태 문장이 가능하다. 이와 같은 수여동사는 다음과 같다.

give	show	teach

They gave me the keys.

→ I was given the keys.

→ The keys were given to me.

Juliet taught me English.

→ I was taught English by Juliet.

→ English was taught to me by Juliet.

2_ 문장 전환할 때 전치사로 **for**를 쓰는 수여동사들은 직접목적어만을 수동태의 주어로 할 수 있는 경우가 많다. 이와 같은 수여동사는 다음과 같다.

buy	cook	find	make

We bought her some flowers.

→ Some flowers were bought for her by us. (O)

→ She was bought some flowers by us. (X)

3_ 수여동사 가운데 **ask**는 간접목적어만을 수동태의 주어로 가질 수 있다.

They asked me some hard questions.

→ I was asked some hard questions by them. (O)

→ Some hard questions were asked to me by them. (X)

Exercises

A 적절한 것을 괄호 안에서 고르시오.

1 The palace was shown (to, of) us yesterday.
2 Many presents were (gave, given) to the poor children.
3 Physics was taught (to, for) me by a famous professor.
4 Delicious sausages were made (to, for) him by a renowned chef.
5 They were (asked, ask) too many questions.
6 Many opportunities were given (to, as) the poor.
7 In some schools, English was (taught, teached) in a new way.

B 밑줄 친 부분이 어법에 맞으면 T, 맞지 않으면 F라고 쓰고 맞게 고치시오.

1 Some apples were <u>give</u> to the children.   ( ) _____
2 The bike was bought <u>for</u> the old man.   ( ) _____
3 We were <u>show</u> a beautiful garden by the lady. ( ) _____
4 The meal was cooked <u>for</u> the guest.   ( ) _____
5 She was taught <u>to</u> Chinese as a child.   ( ) _____
6 Tasty foods were <u>make</u> for the volunteers.   ( ) _____
7 We were given <u>to</u> a rare chance   ( ) _____

C 다음 글의 밑줄 친 부분 중, 어법상 틀린 것은?

Do you know why Americans say that something is ① composed "of" something else? Why do they ② use "of" instead of "from" or "by"? Was the word of given ③ to a special meaning? Or was the expression ④ taught in school for a long time? The real reason is that here the word of means "out of." So Americans believe that something is ⑤ made "out of" something else. Got it?

Form

> **1** The story **was believed to** be entirely made up.
> Melanie **was considered** the best teacher in America.
>
> **2** The lazy boy **was made to** do his homework.
>
> **3** Britney **was seen playing** the piano beautifully.

Meaning & Use

1_ 불완전타동사가 구성하는 문장을 5형식 문형이라고 하는데, 불완전타동사의 목적어를 주어로 하여 수동태를 만들 수 있다. 불완전타동사가 대개 to부정사를 목적격보어로 취하기 때문에 "be＋과거분사" 다음에 to부정사가 오는 경우가 종종 있다. 목적적보어에 해당하는 to부정사가 "to be 명사[형용사]"인 경우에는 to be가 생략될 수 있다.

They expected Hillary to win the election.

→ Hillary was expected to win the election.

They considered him (to be) a superb teacher.

→ He was considered (to be) a superb teacher.

2_ 사역동사인 make이 수동태로 쓰이는 경우에는 본래 목적격보어가 원형부정사라 하더라도 to부정사로 바뀌어야 함에 주의해야 한다.

They made him work very hard.

→ He was made to work very hard. (O)

→ He was made work very hard. (X)

3_ 지각동사도 수동태로 쓰이는 경우에 목적격보어가 원형부정사였다면 to부정사로 바뀌어야 하지만, 현재분사를 활용하는 것이 일반적이다.

We saw the boat flip over in the water.

→ The boat was seen to flip over in the water. (O)

→ The boat was seen flip over in the water. (X)

They heard the singer playing the cello.

→ The singer was heard playing the cello. (O)

→ The singer was heard play the cello. (X)

Exercises

A 적절한 것을 괄호 안에서 고르시오.

1 The animal was thought (be, to be) extinct for years.

2 The rumor was found (to be, be) entirely false.

3 The poor children were made (overwork, to overwork).

4 They were seen (to play, play) chess.

5 He was thought (to be, be) one of the greatest writers of all time.

6 The product was expected (sell, to sell) like hot cakes.

7 The famous violinist was heard (play, playing) the piano.

B 밑줄 친 부분이 어법에 맞으면 T, 맞지 않으면 F라고 쓰고 맞게 고치시오.

1 The woman was kept <u>awake</u> by the sound
of dogs.   (   ) _____

2 Many people were made <u>take</u> part in
the event.   (   ) _____

3 The well-known actor was seen <u>dating</u>
a woman.   (   ) _____

4 The runner was expected <u>win</u>
one million dollars.   (   ) _____

5 Angelina Jolie was considered <u>a heroine</u>.   (   ) _____

6 A few students were made <u>to enter</u> the race. (   ) _____

7 The band was heard <u>play</u> loud music.   (   ) _____

C 다음 글의 밑줄 친 부분 중, 어법상 틀린 것은?

Unfortunately, many people are made ①to overwork these days. Their
work is expected ②give benefit to their employers. But that is not the case.
If workers ③continue to overwork, their health will become worse. In many
cases, their ill health ④leads to many different diseases. When these kinds
of things happen, the employers should pay for their treatment. In this
sense, it is not a good idea to force workers ⑤to overwork.

완료 및 진행형 수동태

Form

> 1 Basketball **has been loved** by many for years.
>   The subject **had** already **been researched** by scientists.
>   The soup **will have been finished** before desert is served.
>
> 2 The TV **is being watched** by the children in the living room.
>   The car **was being driven** to the supermarket yesterday.

Meaning & Use

1_ 완료형 수동태는 다음 세 가지 형식으로 쓰인다.

> 현재완료+수동태 = 「have[has] + been + 과거분사」
> 과거완료+수동태 = 「had + been + 과거분사」
> 미래완료+수동태 = 「will + have + been + 과거분사」

The mail has not been delivered to this area yet.

The dogs had been taken care of by the neighbors.

Your English will have been perfected by the time you go to college.

2_ 진행형 수동태는 크게 다음 두 가지 형식으로 쓰인다.

> 현재진행형 + 수동태 = 「am[are, is] + being + 과거분사」
> 과거진행형 + 수동태 = 「was[were] + being + 과거분사」

The house is being painted a different color.

The cats were being chased by the dogs.

Key point_ 진행형 수동태의 형태

학교 내신시험에서는 진행형 수동태의 형태가 「am[are, is]+being+과거분사」라는 점을 종종 출제한다. 진행형 수동태가 이와 같은 형태가 되는 것은 완료형 수동태와 마찬가지로 영어에서는 시제(tense)가 태(voice)보다 더 우선시되기 때문이다. 「am[are, is]+being+과거분사」에서 "am[are, is] being"은 현재진행형이다. 반면, "being+과거분사"는 수동태이다.

The chicken is being roasted in the oven. (O)

The chicken is roasted being in the oven. (X)

Exercises

A 적절한 것을 괄호 안에서 고르시오.

1 The painting will (have, had) been finished by next week.

2 The mail is (been, being) checked daily.

3 The beds have (being, been) made by the maid.

4 The soup is (being, been) eaten by the customers.

5 The park had (been, being) cleaned by volunteers.

6 The plane was (being, been) flown to Japan.

7 The present had (been, being) wrapped in newspaper.

B 밑줄 친 부분이 어법에 맞으면 T, 맞지 않으면 F라고 쓰고 맞게 고치시오.

1 The television hasn't <u>been turned</u> on
at all recently.   (   ) _____

2 The project will <u>had</u> been finished
before the deadline.   (   ) _____

3 The shots were <u>being</u> fired by the police.   (   ) _____

4 His injuries had <u>being</u> treated at the hospital. (   ) _____

5 The lemonade is being <u>poured</u> into glasses.   (   ) _____

6 The rats are <u>been</u> chased by the chefs.   (   ) _____

7 The orange juice is being <u>spill</u> all over
the place.   (   ) _____

C 다음 글의 밑줄 친 부분 중, 어법상 틀린 것은?

New inventions are ① <u>been</u> made every day. Some of them will help us
② <u>live</u> better lives. But others will have been ③ <u>forgotten</u> soon. We need to
remember, however, that those inventions have ④ <u>been</u> tested so many
times. The inventors have shed blood, sweat, and tears to make their
inventions. Before the inventions are available, the inventors want to
make sure that they will meet the needs of ordinary people. Despite these
efforts, their attempts ⑤ <u>sometimes</u> fail.

Form

1 The room was **filled with** balloons for the birthday party.

2 Everyone was **bored with** the long lecture.

3 These days, many people are **interested in** learning Chinese.

4 Many teachers were **surprised at** the results.

5 Most parents were **concerned about** the new policy.

Meaning & Use

1_ 수동태의 형식을 취하면서도 행위자를 나타낼 때 by 이외의 전치사를 쓰는 표현들이 있다. 이 가운데 cover와 fill은 「be covered [filled] with ~」이라는 형태로 "~로 덮여 [가득 차] 있다"는 뜻을 나타낸다.

The lake was covered with snow.

This book is filled with fascinating stories.

2_ bore, delight, disappoint, satisfy는 「be -ed with ···」이라는 형태로 각각 "···에 지겨워하다" "···에 기뻐하다" "···에 실망하다" "···에 만족하다"라는 뜻을 나타낸다. delighted와 disappointed 다음에는 전치사로 at이 올 수 있다.

Miranda was delighted with her new notebook computer.

The young scientist was disappointed with the test results.

The audience was satisfied with the performance.

3_ interest는 「be interested in ~」이라는 형태로 "~에 관심이 있다"는 뜻을 나타낸다.

As a kid, I was interested in learning how to ride a horse.

4_ excite, frighten, surprise는 「be -ed at ···」이라는 형태로 각각 "···에 흥분하다" "···를 무서워하다" "···에 놀라다"는 뜻을 나타낸다. frightened 다음에는 전치사로 of가 올 수 있다.

All the students were excited at the coming winter vacation.

Many boys are frightened of spiders.

5_ concern과 worry는 「be -ed about ···」이라는 형태로 각각 "···에 대해 우려하다" "···에 대해 걱정하다"라는 뜻을 나타낸다.

Jessica was worried about the safety of her daughter.

Exercises

A 적절한 것을 괄호 안에서 고르시오.

1 The mountain was covered (of, with) ice and snow.

2 Most children were bored (with, at) the boring lesson.

3 The boss was disappointed (at, of) what he had done.

4 A lot of citizens were satisfied (of, with) the progress.

5 Because I want to travel abroad, I am interested (with, in) learning English.

6 Some people are frightened (of, with) water.

7 Many politicians were concerned (about, of) the new law.

B 밑줄 친 부분이 어법에 맞으면 T, 맞지 않으면 F라고 쓰고 맞게 고치시오.

1 Her new book is <u>fill</u> with errors. ( ) _____

2 The child was delighted <u>of</u> his new toy. ( ) _____

3 Many students were disappointed <u>with</u> what he said. ( ) _____

4 Most customers were satisfied <u>of</u> the service. ( ) _____

5 Lizzy was <u>interesting</u> in learning magic. ( ) _____

6 Everybody was surprised <u>at</u> the shocking news. ( ) _____

7 Nobody was worried <u>with</u> the consequences. ( ) _____

C 다음 글의 밑줄 친 부분 중, 어법상 틀린 것은?

These days, so many people are ① interested in stem cell research. This is because they believe that it can cure many different diseases. By ② using stem cells, medical scientists will probably replace old organs with new ones, which is almost the same as curing diseases. Of course, in order to ③ do that, they need to develop stem cells that will grow to be new organs. In ④ doing so, scientists take stem cells from embryos. Some people are ⑤ concerned of that practice. This is because they believe that it is the same as killing humans. Well, what do you think?

Chapter Review

A   잘못된 곳을 고치시오.

1   The famous actors were see by the crowd of people outside.

2   The bank was robbed from thousands of dollars yesterday.

3   Some furniture was steal by the young children.

4   Surprisingly, the big house was sold of the beggar on the street.

5   In fact, the uniform was wore by a famous athlete.

6   I was given to a present by a young student.

7   The apples were bought of the sick child.

8   She was asked of very private questions.

9   The recording studio was shown of us by the manager.

10   The turkey was cooked to the sick mother.

11   The President was expected arrive soon.

12   Many citizens were made build the bridge.

13   The robber was seen break into his house.

14   Erica Kim was considered be one of the greatest writers in the world.

15   The musician was heard sing her favorite song.

16   The soup is been made in the kitchen.

17   The music had being played by a famous pianist.

18   The telegraph had been using before Bell invented the telephone.

19   Mathematics has being studied for centuries.

20   The baby is being took care of by a babysitter.

21   The coast was filled about a larger number of people.

22   Everybody was delight at the prospect of victory.

23   Many young people are interesting in learning how to bungee-jump.

24   Some people are frightened with heights.

25   Many teachers were concerned at the new grading system.

B (A), (B), (C)의 각 괄호 안에서 어법에 맞는 표현을 골라 짝지은 것으로 가장 적절한 것은?

Can school life be (A) [enjoy / enjoyed] by students? Well, what do you think? Has your school gone on an excursion to any famous place? For example, have you ever (B) [been / being] to Niagara Falls? And have you ever (C) [been / being] invited to a prom? By the way, do you know what a prom is? In fact, it has been enjoyed by many American students. Finally, does your school hold an annual festival? Anyway, welcome back to school!

	(A)	(B)	(C)
①	enjoy	being	been
②	enjoyed	been	being
③	enjoyed	been	been
④	enjoy	been	being
⑤	enjoyed	being	being

C 다음 글의 밑줄 친 부분 중, 어법상 틀린 것은?

When I came back to my hometown, it was ① being attacked by aliens. I was so ② surprising! I didn't know what to do. After a while, I found out that their spaceships had ③ been made of gold and silver. Their weapons had been ④ developed for so many years. The weapons developed by my villagers were not as good as theirs. Therefore, most of them just tried to flee from the village. Unfortunately, however, they were ⑤ being chased by the bad aliens.

Chapter Review

D 다음 밑줄 친 부분에 가장 적절한 것을 고르시오.

1 The famous actor is _____ to almost everyone in the nation.
   a. knew   b. know
   c. knowing   d. known

2 Surprisingly, the local bank was _____ many times.
   a. rob   b. robs
   c. robbed   d. robbing

3 In fact, the shoes were _____ by the prince.
   a. worn   b. wore
   c. wear   d. wearing

4 Unfortunately, the book was _____ in broken English.
   a. write   b. written
   c. wrote   d. writing

5 The movement was _____ by a patriotic girl.
   a. lead   b. leading
   c. leads   d. led

6 A special book was given _____ me by the excellent teacher.
   a. with   b. to
   c. of   d. about

7 Big meals were made _____ the poor children.
   a. of   b. to
   c. at   d. for

8 He was _____ an embarrassing question.
   a. ask   b. asks
   c. asked   d. to asking

9 Biology was _____ to us by a famous professor.
   a. teach   b. teaching
   c. teaches   d. taught

10 New computers were _____ for new employees.
   a. buy   b. buying
   c. bought   d. buys

11 She was believed _____ the best athlete of all time.
a. be   b. to be
c. to being   d. is

12 Some participants were made _____.
a. overwork   b. overworks
c. to overworked   d. to overwork

13 The doctor was seen _____ bad things to the patient.
a. do   b. did
c. doing   d. done

14 The treasure was considered _____ worth $1 million.
a. be   b. to be
c. to being   d. is

15 Many young women were made _____ the army.
a. join   b. joins
c. joined   d. to join

16 The newspaper was _____ read daily in the Johnson household.
a. been   b. is
c. being   d. are

17 Rudy has _____ followed by her secret admirer.
a. being   b. had
c. having   d. been

18 The classroom is being _____ by the custodian.
a. clean   b. cleaned
c. cleans   d. cleaning

19 The river was filled _____ polluted materials.
a. of   b. to
c. at   d. with

20 We were _____ in mastering the English language.
a. interesting   b. interested
c. interest   d. interests

Chapter 4

조동사

가능·능력의 조동사 can/could/may

Form

1 Learning English **can be** fun.
The sky **cannot get** any darker than this.

2 That **may be** a possible solution.
That **could be** a possible solution.

3 The train **can travel** up to 100 miles per hour.
She **could speak** Japanese quite well.

4 They **were able to swim** in the river.

Meaning & Use

1_ 어떤 일이 가능하다는 것을 나타낼 때는 「can+동사원형」으로 표현한다. 반면 어떤 일이 가능하지 않다는 것을 나타낼 때는 「cannot+동사원형」으로 표현한다.
Visiting China can give you an insight into its history.
Earning a lot of money cannot make you happy.

2_ 확신은 못하지만 어떤 일이 가능하다고 생각할 때는 「may+동사원형」또는 「could+ 동사원형」으로 표현한다. 「might+동사원형」도 같은 뜻을 나타낸다.
Michelle may be a millionaire. = Michelle could be a millionaire.

3_ 「can+동사원형」은 능력을 나타낼 수 있다. 반면 「could+동사원형」은 과거의 일반적인 능력을 나타낸다.
Fred can play the flute very beautifully. / Sarah could play chess quite well.

4_ 「was [were] able to+동사원형」은 과거의 특정한 상황에서 어떤 일을 실제로 할 수 있었음을 뜻한다. 반면 「could+동사원형」에는 이런 쓰임새가 없다.
They were able to swim in the river.

Key point_ 조동사의 결합

TEPS 등의 어학능력시험에서는 조동사가 서로 이어져서 쓰일 수 없다는 점을 종종 출제한다. 예컨대 "will can" 이나 "can will" 과 같은 결합은 불가능하다. 이런 경우에는 "will be able to" 로 표현해야 한다.
We will be able to attend the reception. (O)
We will can attend the reception. (X)

A 적절한 것을 괄호 안에서 고르시오.

1 Chris can (shoot, shot) the basketball with just one hand.

2 Most students can't (understood, understand) what the teacher is saying.

3 I (can, may can) buy you dinner anytime you want.

4 Some people think the beggar could (is, be) a billionaire.

5 Susie could (to play, play) the cello beautifully.

6 The President was able (to attend, attend) the party.

7 Scientists (will can, will be able to) find the answer.

B 밑줄 친 부분이 어법에 맞으면 T, 맞지 않으면 F라고 쓰고 맞게 고치시오.

1 I can't <u>go</u> out tonight because I have to study. ( ) _____

2 He can <u>played</u> basketball excellently. ( ) _____

3 You can <u>seeing</u> the homes of celebrities in Hollywood. ( ) _____

4 That might <u>been</u> a disaster. ( ) _____

5 Jenny could <u>playing</u> tennis quite well. ( ) _____

6 We were able to <u>make</u> it to the party. ( ) _____

7 He <u>can may</u> be a murderer. ( ) _____

C 다음 글의 밑줄 친 부분 중, 어법상 틀린 것은?

Do you like butterflies? I like them a lot. They are so beautiful, don't you think? Sadly for me, most butterflies can ①<u>live</u> just for two to fourteen days. Some butterflies can ②<u>survived</u> for eleven months. Wow! That's a long time, isn't it? Do you know ③<u>how fast a butterfly can fly</u>? The fastest butterflies can fly at 50 kilometers per hour. They move ④<u>faster</u> than a child on a bicycle. But the slowest butterflies can fly at 8 kilometers per hour. For butterflies to fly, their body temperature needs to be over 30°C (86°F). Isn't that ⑤<u>amazing</u>?

허락의 조동사 can/could/may

Form

> 1 You can have the last cupcake on the table.
>   You **cannot go** to the party tonight because you must do your homework.
>
> 2 We **could play** with the toys any time we wanted to.
>   We **could not play** together last night because our parents wouldn't let us.
>
> 3 **May** I **borrow** your car tomorrow for work?
>   You **may not play** computer games all night long.
>
> 4 You **will be allowed to go** to basketball camp this summer.

Meaning & Use

1 _ "~해도 된다"는 허락의 의미는 「can+동사원형」으로 표현한다. "~할 수 없다"는 의미는 「cannot+동사원형」으로 표현한다.

You can take a break in fifteen minutes.

You cannot smoke in this restaurant.

2 _ "~해도 되었다"는 과거의 허락의 의미는 「could+동사원형」으로 표현한다. "~할 수 없었다"는 의미는 「could not+동사원형」으로 표현한다.

I could watch television for a few minutes.

The dog couldn't come inside the house.

3 _ "—해도 된다"는 허락의 의미를 보다 정중한 상황에서 나타내는 경우에는 「may+동사원형」이라는 형태를 활용한다. 반면 "~할 수 없다"는 의미를 보다 정중한 상황에서 나타내는 경우에는 「may not+동사원형」이라는 형태를 활용한다.

You may go to the restrooms during break.

We may not enter the forbidden areas of the temple.

4 _ 조동사 can이나 may는 다른 조동사와 결합하여 쓸 수 없기 때문에 그런 경우에는 「조동사+be allowed to+동사원형」이라는 형태를 써야 한다.

The students will be allowed to wear whatever they like. (O)

The students will may wear whatever they like. (X)

Exercises

A 적절한 것을 괄호 안에서 고르시오.

1 You may not (talking, talk) on your cell phone during class.

2 The employees can (had, have) only one hour for lunch.

3 Pregnant women cannot (enter, entering) this swimming pool.

4 We may not (trespass, trespasses) into private property.

5 I couldn't (went, go) outside after 9 p.m. when I was a child.

6 You cannot (say, saying) such rude things to your grandfather.

7 He couldn't (plays, play) golf with his parents because he was grounded.

B 밑줄 친 부분이 어법에 맞으면 T, 맞지 않으면 F라고 쓰고 맞게 고치시오.

1 You can <u>have</u> just one slice of pie for dessert. ( ) _____

2 You may not <u>drank</u> alcohol in public in America. ( ) _____

3 Children cannot <u>riding</u> that scary roller coaster. ( ) _____

4 You cannot <u>takes</u> more than three days' vacation. ( ) _____

5 Of course, you may <u>had</u> seconds. ( ) _____

6 You can <u>take</u> a few days off from work. ( ) _____

7 All the students <u>can wil</u>l attend the reception. ( ) _____

C 다음 글의 밑줄 친 부분 중, 어법상 틀린 것은?

The boy has trouble with his parents. He wants to be an artist, but his parents want him ① to be a lawyer. In other words, the boy cannot ② pursued his dream. The girl tells him that he ③ may have both jobs. The boy disagrees. He thinks that he needs ④ to listen to his heart. I believe that the boy's idea is a better way to solve the problem. It is very difficult to study both art and law. And law is not what the boy wants to study in the first place. Eventually his parents ⑤ will understand him.

Form

1 **Could you give** me a ride home after school?

2 **Would you help** me move the piano into the living room?
Will you please **water** the garden?

3 **Can you pass** me the salt please?

4 **Would you mind** closing the door?

Meaning & Use

1_ "~해 주시겠어요?"라는 정중한 요청은 「Could＋you＋동사원형...?」으로 나타낸다. 이처럼 조동사의 과거형을 쓰는 경우 상대에 대한 배려를 뜻하기 때문에 매우 정중한 표현이 된다.
Could you take care of my dog while I'm gone on vacation?

2_ 이에 반해 「Would＋you＋동사원형...?」이나 「Will＋you＋동사원형...?」은 대개 명령을 내릴 수 있는 입장에 있는 사람이 쓰는 표현이다. Would를 쓰는 것이 보다 정중한 표현이다.
Would you go to the bookstore and pick up a few cookbooks for me?
Will you change the baby's diapers?

3_ 상대에게 간단한 요청을 하는 경우에는 「Can＋you＋동사원형...?」으로 나타낸다.
Can you give me a call tonight?

4_ 요청을 나타내는 다른 형태로 「Would＋you＋mind＋-ing...?」를 들 수 있다.
Would you mind rewriting this paragraph please?

Key point_ mind＋-ing

학교 내신시험이나 TEPS 등의 각종 어학시험에서는 「Would＋you＋mind...?」라는 표현에서 mind 다음에 -ing가 와야 한다는 점을 자주 출제한다. 이 표현이 어떤 일을 앞으로 해 줄 것을 요청하는 표현이기 때문에 mind 다음에 미래를 나타내는 to부정사가 와야 하는 것으로 생각하기 쉽지만, 이때 mind가 "싫어하다, 꺼리다"는 뜻이어서 반드시 -ing가 와야 함에 유의해야 한다.
Would you mind waiting a second? (O)
Would you mind to wait a second? (X)

Exercises

A 적절한 것을 괄호 안에서 고르시오.

1 Could you (done, do) me a big favor, please?

2 Would you (take, taking) me to the drugstore this afternoon?

3 Can you (passed, pass) me the salt, please?

4 Would you mind (to open, opening) the window a little bit?

5 Could you (buying, buy) me a new bicycle for Christmas?

6 Will you (reply, replying) to my message by tomorrow afternoon?

7 Would you mind (lending, to lend) me five dollars?

B 밑줄 친 부분이 어법에 맞으면 T, 맞지 않으면 F라고 쓰고 맞게 고치시오.

1 Could you <u>cover</u> me at work this Friday?　( )　＿＿＿＿＿＿＿

2 Will you <u>taking</u> out the garbage?　( )　＿＿＿＿＿＿＿

3 Can you <u>sent</u> me the information
by tomorrow?　( )　＿＿＿＿＿＿＿

4 Would you mind <u>to help</u> me clean the house?　( )　＿＿＿＿＿＿＿

5 Will you <u>stayed</u> longer after work?　( )　＿＿＿＿＿＿＿

6 Could you <u>given</u> me some medicine?　( )　＿＿＿＿＿＿＿

7 Would you mind <u>picking</u> up some sugar?　( )　＿＿＿＿＿＿＿

C 다음 글의 밑줄 친 부분 중, 어법상 틀린 것은?

One day, a student ① <u>said</u> to me, "Would you mind ② <u>to help</u> me make our school beautiful?" I thought that ③ <u>was</u> a wonderful idea. To be frank with you, I had never ④ <u>thought</u> of such an issue. Of course, as a teacher, I often said to the students, "Will you please clean the classroom?" But I had never thought cleaning might be part of making our school beautiful. So, I was deeply ⑤ <u>impressed</u> by that idea.

Form

1 We must try our best to win the game.
   We have to fight with all our strength.

2 I had to do my own laundry.

3 We should leave before the sun goes down.
   You ought to go to the library and study.

4 You must not go to the party tonight.
   You don't have to go to the party tonight.

Meaning & Use

1_ "~하지 않으면 안 된다"는 의무는 「must+동사원형」으로 나타낸다. 같은 뜻을 나타내는 표현에는 「have [has] to+동사원형」이 있다. 주어가 3인칭 단수일 때는 has to를, 나머지 경우에는 have to를 쓴다는 점에 유의해야 한다.

You must get there by ten in the morning.

You have to come out of your room.

My father has to mow the lawn every Saturday.

2_ "~했어야만 했다"는 과거의 의무는 「had to+동사원형」으로 나타낸다.

My mother had to cook dinner every night.

3_ "~해야 한다"는 경미한 의무는 「should+동사원형」 또는 「ought to+동사원형」으로 나타낸다. 특히 「ought to+동사원형」에서 to를 뺄 수 없다는 점에 주의해야 한다.

We should take a shower after we play basketball.

You ought to shave your beard before your job interview. (O)

You ought shave your beard before your job interview. (X)

4_ must와 have to의 부정형이 서로 다른 의미를 나타냄에 특히 유의해야 한다. must의 부정형인 「must not+동사원형」은 "~해서는 안 된다"는 금지의 의미를, have to의 부정형인 「don't[doesn't] have to+동사원형」은 "~할 필요 없다"는 의미를 나타낸다.

You must not treat your sister unfairly.

You don't have to feed the fish every day.

Exercises

A   적절한 것을 괄호 안에서 고르시오.

1   They (musted, had to) leave the house.

2   Fred (has, have) to finish eating his breakfast.

3   The employee doesn't (has, have) to work on Saturdays.

4   You (don't, doesn't) have to check your mail every day.

5   They (has, have) to take care of their baby.

6   You ought (to take, take) the dog out for walks.

7   You should (to think, think) about your future.

B   밑줄 친 부분이 어법에 맞으면 T, 맞지 않으면 F라고 쓰고 맞게 고치시오.

1   We <u>had to pack</u> our things for our vacation.   ( ) _____

2   Everyone <u>have to</u> brush their teeth.   ( ) _____

3   You <u>ought come</u> back home soon.   ( ) _____

4   You <u>have to go</u> to class every day.   ( ) _____

5   We <u>should to</u> give the dog healthy treats..   ( ) _____

6   We had to <u>stretched</u> for the big football game. ( ) _____

7   You <u>don't have to</u> worry about it.   ( ) _____

C   다음 글의 밑줄 친 부분 중, 어법상 틀린 것은?

Do you know ① <u>what manatees are</u>? Just like whales, they are sea mammals. In fact, they look like whales. But they move very, very slowly. So they often lose their lives ② <u>because of</u> collisions with boats and ships. They also lose their lives because of water pollution. Sometimes they lose their lives because of waste materials ③ <u>thrown</u> away by people. Because manatees are very shy, touching and feeding them ④ <u>can move</u> them to dangerous areas. So we ⑤ <u>must to</u> be very careful to protect manatees.

충고의 조동사 should/ought to/had better

Form

1 You **should go** see the doctor for that wound.
   You **should not wear** too much perfume.

2 You **ought to go** see the doctor for that wound.
   He **ought not to** play video games.

3 You **had better read** the paper before you leave for work.
   You **had better not leave** now.

Meaning & Use

1_ 경미한 의무를 나타내는 「should+동사원형」은 어떤 일을 해야 하는지에 대한 충고를 나타낼 수 있다. 어떤 일을 하지 말아야 한다고 충고할 때는 「should not+동사원형」으로 표현한다. "should not"은 "shouldn't"으로 축약하여 나타낼 수 있다.

You should apologize for what you said to her earlier.
You shouldn't drive fast on the highway.

2_ 「should+동사원형」과 마찬가지로 「ought to+동사원형」도 충고의 의미를 나타낼 수 있다. 어떤 일을 하지 말아야 한다고 충고할 때는 「ought not to+동사원형」이라는 형태를 쓰는데, "ought not"은 "oughtn't으로 축약할 수 있다.

Billy ought to play his violin more quietly.
You oughtn't to bring a lot of food for this trip.

3_ "~하는 편이 낫다"는 뜻의 「had better+동사원형」도 충고를 나타낼 수 있다. 특히 "~하지 않는 편이 낫다"는 뜻은 「had better not+동사원형」으로 표현해야 함에 주의해야 한다. 「had not better+동사원형」으로는 쓸 수 없다.

You had better park your car in a safe area of the neighborhood.
You had better not stay longer.

Key point_ **had better**의 부정형

학교 내신시험에서는 「had better+동사원형」의 부정이 「had better not+동사원형」이라는 사항을 자주 출제한다. 이처럼 not이 had better 다음에 와야 하는 것은 had better 전체가 하나의 조동사 역할을 하기 때문이다. 절대로 had not better와 같이 쓸 수 없다는 점을 기억해야 한다.

You had better not go camping in this rain. (O)
You had not better go camping in this rain. (X)

Exercises

A 적절한 것을 괄호 안에서 고르시오.

1 You (have, had) better take your medicine now.

2 Fred (should, ought) pay more attention in class.

3 You had better (to use, use) bug spray before you go out into the woods.

4 We ought (get, to get) the clothes inside before it rains.

5 Your brother ought (not to, to not) help you with your homework.

6 Tim had (not better, better not) cut his hair.

7 She had better (wear, wearing) gloves out in the snow.

B 밑줄 친 부분이 어법에 맞으면 T, 맞지 않으면 F라고 쓰고 맞게 고치시오.

1 You <u>should use</u> a pen to fill out the application.   ( ) _____

2 You <u>had not better</u> go to that store.   ( ) _____

3 You <u>ought leave</u> your dog behind for this trip. ( ) _____

4 Dorothy <u>ought to not</u> call her boyfriend.   ( ) _____

5 You <u>have better</u> wear boots.   ( ) _____

6 Darryl <u>should stop</u> playing his saxophone in the alley.   ( ) _____

7 You ought <u>use to</u> deodorant once in a while.   ( ) _____

C 다음 글의 밑줄 친 부분 중, 어법상 틀린 것은?

We usually don't like people who are different from us in some way. Their skin color ① may be different. They ② can be from different countries. They may look very different from us. In any case, we ③ ought not look down on them. We ④ should respect them as people. Just like us, they have feelings. Just like us, they have dreams. Just like us, they want to be happy. So, if we want them to respect us, we ⑤ ought to respect them first. Respect brings respect, and when we respect each other, we can live much more happy lives.

추측의 조동사 must/can't/may/might

Form

> 1 This **must be** a better decision.
>
> 2 She **can't be** the queen of England.
>
> 3 The cave **may be** dangerous.
> They **might** still **be** working on the project.

Meaning & Use

1_ "~임에 틀림없다"는 강한 추측은 「must+동사원형」으로 나타낸다.

The girls must be upstairs in their room.

2_ "~일 리가 없다"는 강한 부정의 추측은 「cannot [can't]+동사원형」으로 나타낸다. 「must not+동사원형」으로 표현할 수 없음에 특히 유의해야 한다.

She must be his sister. ↔ She can't be his sister.

3_ "~일지도 모른다"는 불확실한 추측은 「may+동사원형」으로 나타낸다. 「might+동사원형」을 쓰면 보다 불확실한 추측을 나타낸다.

My parents may still be eating at the restaurant.

The bus might be headed for Chicago.

Key point_ **must not vs. can't**

학교 내신시험에서는 「must not+동사원형」이 "~하지 않으면 안 된다"는 뜻의 must의 부정형이지 "~임에 틀림없다"는 뜻의 must의 부정형이 아니라는 사항을 종종 출제한다. "~임에 틀림없다"는 뜻의 must의 부정형은 「can't+동사원형」임에 유의해야 한다.

She must be his daughter. ↔ She can't be his daughter.

≠ She must not be his daughter.

Exercises

A 적절한 것을 괄호 안에서 고르시오.

1   He must (be, been) studying for the big test right now.
2   This (can't, oughtn't) be the only way to do this problem.
3   The chicken (maybe, may be) ready to eat.
4   The dog (must, had not better) like to chase cats.
5   He (had not better, can't) be going home already.
6   Judging from its shell, it (must, had better) be a tortoise.
7   It (can't, must not) be night already.

B 밑줄 친 부분이 어법에 맞으면 T, 맞지 않으면 F라고 쓰고 맞게 고치시오.

1   It <u>might be</u> poisonous, so don't touch it.   ( ) _____

2   The house <u>must not</u> be over a hundred
    years old.   ( ) _____

3   It <u>can be not</u> raining outside.   ( ) _____

4   The clothes <u>must be</u> dry by now.   ( ) _____

5   She <u>may taking</u> her lunch break right now.   ( ) _____

6   That car <u>must not be</u> the governor's.   ( ) _____

7   He <u>must like</u> fruit.   ( ) _____

C 다음 글의 밑줄 친 부분 중, 어법상 틀린 것은?

Have you ever ① <u>seen</u> panda cubs? They are so cute! Mother pandas are black and white, but panda cubs are white. Unfortunately, they ② <u>cannot see</u> for about seven weeks. And they are so small. Sometimes I feel like ③ <u>touching</u> their bodies. Did you know that they have no fur? I guess their bodies ④ <u>maybe</u> slippery. Anyway, I want to touch them. And did you know that they are disappearing? A lot of people are trying to kill them. How ⑤ <u>can</u> they do that? Don't they want to see these cute animals anymore?

조동사 + have + 과거분사

1 Ted **must have forgotten** his keys at home.
   She **cannot have been** there.

2 The plane **may have landed** already in Paris.

3 We **should have eaten** at a different restaurant.
   We **shouldn't have taken** the shortcut.

Meaning & Use

1_ 「must have+과거분사」는 "~했음에 틀림없다"는 뜻을 나타낸다. 이에 반해, 「cannot have+과거분사」는 "~했을 리가 없다"는 뜻을 나타낸다. 각 형태에 따른 쓰임새를 정확히 익혀두어야 한다.

We must have left the door unlocked!

↔ We cannot have left the door unlocked!

2_ 「may have+과거분사」는 "~했을지도 모른다"는 뜻을 나타낸다.

We may have put too much salt in the chicken.

3_ 「should have+과거분사」는 "~했어야 했는데"라는 과거에 대한 유감의 뜻을 나타낸다. 「shouldn't have+과거분사」는 "~하지 말았어야 했는데"라는 뜻을 나타낸다. 전자는 과거에 특정한 일을 했어야 했는데, 사실은 하지 않았다는 의미이고, 후자는 과거에 특정한 일을 하지 말았어야 했는데, 사실은 했다는 의미이다.

You should have brought an umbrella with you.

You shouldn't have told him about it.

Key point_ must have+과거분사 vs. should have+과거분사

TEPS 등의 어학시험에서는 「must have+과거분사」와 「should have+과거분사」가 쓰임새가 다르다는 점을 자주 출제한다. must와 should에 둘 다 "의무"의 쓰임새가 있기 때문에, "have+과거분사"와 결합한 형태가 똑같은 뜻을 나타낸다고 생각하기 쉬운데, 그렇지 않다는 점에 특히 유의해야 한다.

He must have eaten enough. ≠ He should have eaten enough.

Exercises

A 적절한 것을 괄호 안에서 고르시오.

1 You (should, must) have made a mistake.

2 I shouldn't have (touching, touched) the poison ivy.

3 He must (had, have) left for home already.

4 The governor should have (pass, passed) the new traffic law.

5 The ship (must, had not better) have sunk into the sea.

6 She (must, should) have paid more attention. That was a terrible mistake.

7 The milkman (had not better, must) have stopped by.

B 밑줄 친 부분이 어법에 맞으면 T, 맞지 않으면 F라고 쓰고 맞게 고치시오.

1 It <u>must have snowed</u> in the mountains. ( ) _____

2 We <u>should had bought</u> a motorcycle. ( ) _____

3 My keys <u>must have fallen</u> out of my pockets. ( ) _____

4 I <u>should have worn</u> sunscreen at the beach. ( ) _____

5 They <u>must have fix</u> the machine. ( ) _____

6 She <u>should has known</u> better. ( ) _____

7 The bus <u>must have come</u> already. ( ) _____

C 다음 글의 밑줄 친 부분 중, 어법상 틀린 것은?

My neighborhood had a lot of problems such as noise pollution, bad manners, and heavy traffic. Other neighborhoods ① <u>must have had</u> similar problems, too. But what I ② <u>couldn't understand</u> was why senior citizens kept silent about important issues. For example, I had never seen old people ③ <u>scold</u> young people for bad manners. Because senior citizens had had a lot of experience, they ④ <u>needed</u> to <u>be</u> actively involved in community matters. They ⑤ <u>must have</u> helped our community to become a better place for all.

Chapter Review

A   잘못된 곳을 고치시오.

1   Sam can may run five miles without taking a break.

2   The store owner will be able reopen her shop soon.

3   They could able to stop by Japan on the way to the United States.

4   Children cannot played outside at night.

5   Students will may enter the teacher's lounge.

6   You are not allow to travel without a passport.

7   Must you pass me the salt, please?

8   Should you pour me a glass of milk?

9   Would you mind to give this note to him?

10   The mother have to make dinner before her kids get home.

11   The counselor ought help students with emotional problems.

12   Citizens must should obey the law.

13   I musted go to the bank and deposit my money.

14   You have better buy new tires for your car.

15   You ought wear cleats when you play soccer.

16   The restaurant should must provide better service to its customers.

17   I had better going home before my mother gets angry.

18   She must can be my boss's daughter.

19   That strange student maybe right.

20   The shirt must should be very, very expensive.

21   Judging from what we've found out, Toby must not be a liar.

22   They must have already leave.

23   They should having attended the show.

24   She must had been a beauty in her day.

25   He should have went with you.

B (A), (B), (C)의 각 괄호 안에서 어법에 맞는 표현을 골라 짝지은 것으로 가장 적절한 것은?

People who support stem cell research (A) [ought / should] think twice. Is it O.K. for us to use the cells of embryos without (B) [thinking / think] about the importance of life? They seem to think that embryos are not humans. But they *are*! Even if they are small, even if they are not like us, even if they do not speak, they are humans. So, we (C) [has / have] to respect them. This means that we should not use them like animals. In fact, using them is killing them. This is wrong. We should stop stem cell research right away!

	(A)	(B)	(C)
①	should	think	has
②	ought	thinking	have
③	ought	think	has
④	should	thinking	have
⑤	ought	thinking	has

C 다음 글의 밑줄 친 부분 중, 어법상 틀린 것은?

Just like a sentence, a paragraph ① must have one main idea. If a paragraph has too many main ideas, your readers will have difficulty ② understanding your point. So, when ③ writing a paragraph, always think about one main idea. If you do not think about it, your writing will not work. This ④ had better sound too easy, but it is not. Remember that ⑤ focusing on one idea is the secret to good writing.

Chapter Review

D 다음 밑줄 친 부분에 가장 적절한 것을 고르시오.

1 I _____ believe the paper is due in one week.
- a. ought
- b. have better
- c. can't
- d. oughtn't

2 We were able _____ the party at her house.
- a. have
- b. to have
- c. having
- d. had

3 You can _____ more at buffets.
- a. eat
- b. to eat
- c. eating
- d. eats

4 Boys _____ not enter the girls' locker room.
- a. have better
- b. ought
- c. may
- d. are allowed

5 The airplane _____ land without the control tower's permission.
- a. wasn't able
- b. couldn't
- c. wasn't allowed
- d. musted

6 The dog is _____ to sleep on the bed.
- a. could
- b. allowed
- c. had
- d. ought

7 _____ you buy me a soccer ball for Christmas?
- a. Ought
- b. Allow
- c. Able
- d. Could

8 Will you please _____ to my message next time?
- a. replied
- b. reply
- c. replying
- d. replies

9 Would you mind _____ me find the way to the police station?
- a. to help
- b. help
- c. helped
- d. helping

10 The doctor _____ to prescribe medicine for all his patients.
- a. has
- b. have
- c. should
- d. allowed

11 We ought _____ care of the dog until its owner gets back.
   a. take   b. took
   c. taking   d. to take

12 You don't _____ to do this absurd thing.
   a. has   b. have
   c. had   d. having

13 You _____ finish your homework before dinner.
   a. have better   b. ought
   c. able to   d. had better

14 You _____ eat these vegetables because they're good for you.
   a. ought   b. should
   c. had   d. able

15 You _____ go bungee jumping.
   a. had not better   b. not had better
   c. had better not   d. better not had

16 This _____ be the hardest decision for her.
   a. ought   b. must
   c. had   d. better

17 He should _____ to school yesterday.
   a. had gone   b. has went
   c. have go   d. have gone

18 The birds _____ have escaped from their cage.
   a. ought   b. must
   c. allowed   d. were able

19 Max must have _____ a brat.
   a. being   b. to be
   c. been   d. be

20 We _____ have eaten so many hamburgers.
   a. ought   b. oughtn't
   c. had   d. shouldn't

Chapter 5

부정사

Form

> 1 **To listen** to music can be relaxing.
>   **It** can be relaxing **to listen** to music.
>
> 2 I **want to buy** a new cell phone soon.
>   **Remember to wash** your face before you go to school.
>
> 3 The key is **to understand** the purpose of the experiment.

Meaning & Use

1 _ 「to + 동사원형」을 to부정사라고 하는데, 명사·형용사·부사 등의 역할을 맡을 수 있다. 명사처럼 쓰일 때 to부정사가 문장의 주어가 될 수 있는데, 이와 같은 경우 대개 to 부정사를 문장 끝으로 보내고 가주어 It을 문장의 처음에 쓴다.

To practice often is helpful. = It is helpful to practice often.
　　　　　　　　　　　　　　　(가주어)　　　　　(진주어)

2 _ to부정사는 동사의 목적어로도 쓰이는데, 동사에 따라서 to부정사만이 목적어로 오는 경우도 있고, to부정사와 동명사(-ing)가 둘 다 목적어로 오는 경우도 있다. to부정사만이 목적어로 오는 중요한 동사는 다음과 같다.

choose	decide	expect	hope	plan	refuse	want

We planned to help him move to his new house.

to부정사와 동명사가 둘 다 목적어로 오는 중요한 동사는 다음과 같다.

begin	continue	hate	like	love	start	forget	regret	remember	try

I love to sing songs.
They tried hard to fulfill their dream.

3 _ to부정사는 be 동사 다음에 와서 주격보어로 쓰일 수도 있다. 이때 주어와 동일한 관계에 놓인다는 점에 주의해야 한다.

His dream is to be a famous dancer.　　　<His dream = to be a famous dancer>

Exercises

A   적절한 것을 괄호 안에서 고르시오.

1   It is very difficult (understand, to understand) the topic.

2   Mary likes (to read, reads) books.

3   I forgot (brought, to bring) my umbrella.

4   They tried (engages, to engage) in thoughtful discussion.

5   Sam hates (to listen, listens) to country music.

6   It is very important (dressed, to dress) properly for an interview.

7   His ambition is (to become, becomes) President of the United States.

B   밑줄 친 부분이 어법에 맞으면 T, 맞지 않으면 F라고 쓰고 맞게 고치시오.

1   It is not necessary <u>to cancel</u> the event.   (   ) _____

2   I hated <u>go</u> to the dentist.   (   ) _____

3   Julie loved <u>watched</u> scary movies.   (   ) _____

4   We wanted <u>visiting</u> you at the hospital.   (   ) _____

5   We tried <u>to playing</u> football in the fifth grade.   (   ) _____

6   Did you remember <u>to take</u> out the trash?   (   ) _____

7   Her favorite hobby is <u>fixes</u> cars.   (   ) _____

C   다음 글의 밑줄 친 부분 중, 어법상 틀린 것은?

Friends for Life is a charity in America. Its people try ① <u>to visit</u> the elderly every weekend. And do you know ② <u>what the people do</u>? They listen to elderly people. They give them dolls. They help them ③ <u>clean their</u> houses. They help them wash their clothes. Do you know what the elderly ④ <u>like best</u>? They like it best when the people at *Friends for Life* listen to their stories. Why? Because elderly people want ⑤ <u>being</u> with someone who cares about them. So, the people at *Friends for Life* are really friends for the elderly.

Form

1 We must think of a way **to save** money.

2 We **are to be** married on October 31.
They **were** never **to meet** again.
Nothing **was to be** heard on the street.

3 The children **seemed to enjoy** the party.

4 As time went by, we **came to like** the school.

Meaning & Use

1_ to부정사는 형용사처럼 명사나 대명사를 수식할 수 있는데, 이때 수식하는 어구 다음에 와야 함에 유의해야 한다.

I have a new dog to play with.

Is there someone to guard the building at night?

2_ "be+to부정사"는 예정, 운명, 가능 등을 나타낸다. 이때 주의할 점은 문장의 주어가 to 부정사와 동일하지 않다는 점이다. 이 점에서 주격보어로 쓰이는 명사적 용법의 to부정사와 다르다.

The ceremony is to be held at the community center. (ceremony ≠ to be held)

The hostages were never to be released. (hostages ≠ to be released)

Her presence was to be felt by everybody. (presence ≠ to be felt)

cf. Her ambition was to become a model. (ambition = to become a model)

3_ to부정사는 불완전자동사인 seem이나 appear의 보어로 쓰일 수 있다. "~한 것 같다" 라는 뜻의 이들 동사가 나타내는 시제와 동일한 때에 대해 말할 때는 "to+동사원형"이라는 형태를, 이전에 대해 말할 때는 "to+have+과거분사" 라는 완료형을 쓴다.

They seem to be tired. = It seems that they are tired.

They seem to have been tired. = It seems that they were [have been] tired.

They seemed to be tired. = It seemed that they were tired.

They seemed to have been tired. = It seemed that they had been tired.

4_ to부정사는 불완전자동사인 come이나 get 다음에 와서 보어로 쓰일 수 있다. "~하게 되다" 라는 뜻을 나타낸다.

Susie got to like Peter.

Exercises

A 적절한 것을 괄호 안에서 고르시오.

1   There's nobody (take, to take) me to school today.

2   We must find a way (opens, to open) the door.

3   I need a TV (to provide, provide) me with news.

4   The play was to (performed, be performed) on the weekend.

5   Her face seemed to be (familiarly, familiar).

6   They seemed to (feel, feeling) much better.

7   He came to (hate, hates) politics.

B 밑줄 친 부분이 어법에 맞으면 T, 맞지 않으면 F라고 쓰고 맞게 고치시오.

1   I need some paper <u>to write</u>.   ( ) _____

2   She brought some salt <u>to add</u> to the soup.   ( ) _____

3   They have a large dog <u>guarded</u> their house.   ( ) _____

4   The students seemed <u>to had made</u> fun of him. ( ) _____

5   They seemed <u>to enjoy</u> the trip.   ( ) _____

6   The students seemed <u>to happy</u>.   ( ) _____

7   Many children came <u>disliked</u> the teacher.   ( ) _____

C 다음 글의 밑줄 친 부분 중, 어법상 틀린 것은?

Do you know ① where Knoebels Amusement Park & Resort is? You may
hear this name for the first time. But it *is* a great place ② to have fun. The
amusement park is ③ located in central Pennsylvania. My favorite
attraction in this amusement park is the Galleon. This "ship" is like the
Conquistador in Lotte World. Many people know this attraction as the
Viking. In a sense, the conquistador and the viking are ④ to be confuse.
Anyway, the Galleon gives me a thrill every time I get on the ship. How
about ⑤ giving it a try?

Form

> 1 We ran **to get** away from the bees.
> 2 Michelle grew up **to be** a scientist.
> 3 We're happy **to be** of service.
> 4 She was wise **to reject** the offer.

Meaning & Use

1 _ to부정사는 부사적으로 쓰여 "~하기 위해서"라는 목적을 나타낼 수 있다.
He's running to catch up with the others.

2 _ to부정사는 "결국 —하게 되다"라는 결과를 나타낼 수 있다. "목적"과의 차이는 "목적"의 to 부정사 앞에는 주어의 의지가 깊이 관여하는 동사가 와야 한다는 점이다. 반면, "결과"의 to 부정사 앞에는 대체로 주어의 의지와 관계없는 동사가 온다.
Her grandmother lived to be ninety. (결과)
We must leave now to catch the train. (목적)

3 _ to부정사는 "~해서 (어떤 감정을 갖게 되다)"라는 감정의 원인을 나타낼 수 있다. 이러한 쓰임새에서는 to부정사 앞에 반드시 감정을 나타내는 말이 온다.
I'm disappointed to know that the Eagles lost the game.

4 _ to부정사는 "~하다니 (어떠어떠하다)"라는 판단의 근거를 나타낼 수 있다. 이때 to부정사 앞에는 사람의 특성을 나타내는 말이 오는 것이 보통이다.
I was foolish to believe what he told me.

Key point _ **to 부정사의 부사적 용법의 구분**

학교 내신시험에서는 to부정사의 부사적 용법 네 가지를 정확히 구별할 것을 요구하는 문제를 종종 출제한다. 네 가지 용법의 차이는 언제나 to부정사 바로 앞에 오는 말을 통해 알 수 있다는 점을 활용하면 된다. "목적"일 때는 의지에 따른 행동이, "결과"일때는 의지와 무관한 상태가, "원인"일 때는 감정을 나타내는 말이, "근거"일 때는 사람의 특성을 나타내는 말이 앞에 온다는 것을 기억할 필요가 있다.

He ran as fast as he could to get there in time. (의지 → 목적)
I'm happy to see you today. (감정 → 원인)
Dorothy was thoughtful to send them a thank–you note. (특성 → 근거)

Exercises

A 적절한 것을 괄호 안에서 고르시오.

1 Lewis bought a new pair of cleats (played, to play) soccer.

2 I'm excited to (meet, meets) you, Mr. Robinson.

3 I changed my clothes (gone, to go) out.

4 Jesicca was foolish (enough to follow, to follow enough) his advice.

5 My mother came in to (checking, check) on me.

6 We swam faster to (gotten, get) away from the shark.

7 He sang (relieved, to relieve) his stress.

B 밑줄 친 부분이 어법에 맞으면 T, 맞지 않으면 F라고 쓰고 맞게 고치시오.

1 We went to the lake <u>went</u> fishing.   ( ) _____

2 The cat is hiding inside the bushes
<u>to avoid</u> the dog.   ( ) _____

3 We were sad <u>saw</u> her go.   ( ) _____

4 We stopped by his house <u>borrows</u>
some sugar.   ( ) _____

5 We were glad <u>to hear</u> that she was safe.   ( ) _____

6 I must go to the store <u>bought</u> groceries.   ( ) _____

7 He was sad <u>misses</u> your performance.   ( ) _____

C 다음 글의 밑줄 친 부분 중, 어법상 틀린 것은?

Did you know that parent hamsters sometimes eat their babies? Can you
① <u>believe</u> that? You see, hamsters are so cute that everyone ② <u>likes</u> them.
How can they do that? Why do they do that? Parent hamsters do that
③ <u>to protect</u> other baby hamsters. Sometimes there are baby hamsters
which cannot ④ <u>survive</u>. They cannot live long and can make other baby
hamsters ill. Perhaps, the parent hamsters feel very sad ⑤ <u>to killing</u> those
hamsters. How strange nature is!

Form

> 1 Lizzy was **too** young **to understand** what her sisters were talking about.
>
> 2 Sue was kind **enough to help** me out.
>   Sue was **so** kind **as to help** me out.
>
> 3 We should do a lot of things **in order to achieve** our goal.
>   We should do a lot of things **so as to achieve** our goal.
>
> 4 I **had no choice but to let** her go.
>
> 5 **To begin with**, it is important to understand the purpose of the project.
>   **To be frank with you**, I made a terrible mistake.

Meaning & Use

1_ "too ~to …"는 "너무 ~해서 …할 수 없다" 또는 "…하기에는 너무 ~하다"라는 뜻을 나타낸다. 대개 "so ~ that can't …"로 전환할 수 있다.

Daniel was too shocked to think clearly.

= Daniel was so shocked that he couldn't think clearly.

2_ "~ enough to …"와 "so ~ as to …"는 "…할 만큼 (충분히) ~한"이라는 뜻을 나타낸다.

James was foolish enough to believe what everybody else said.

= James was so foolish as to believe what everybody else said.

3_ "in order to ~"와 "so as to ~"는 "~하기 위해서"라는 뜻을 나타낸다. 대개 "so that S + can ~"이나 "in order that S + can ~"으로 전환할 수 있다.

We worked harder in order to prepare for the exam.

≒ We worked harder so as to prepare for the exam.

≒ We worked harder so[in order] that we could prepare for the exam.

4_ "have no choice but to ~"는 "~하지 않을 수 없다"는 뜻을 나타낸다. but 다음에 to부정사가 와야 함에 유의해야 한다.

We had no choice but to lend him some money.

5_ "to begin with"은 "우선 첫째로"라는 뜻을, "to be frank with you"는 "솔직히 말하면"이란 뜻을 나타낸다.

To begin with, you need to learn the basic of writing.

To be frank with you, I'm broke.

Exercises

A 적절한 것을 괄호 안에서 고르시오.

1 Kate was (too shy, shy enough) to talk with strangers.

2 Mary was (too young, young enough) to go to school.

3 Michael was (too foolish, foolish enough) to believe such nonsense.

4 We listen to music (in order to relax, so relax as to).

5 I will drive there tomorrow (so as to see, so as see to) if it's open.

6 They had no choice but (to leave, leaving) their village.

7 Michelle had no choice but (to dump, dumped) Tom.

B 밑줄 친 부분이 어법에 맞으면 T, 맞지 않으면 F 라고 쓰고 맞게 고치시오.

1 Alice was <u>enough brave</u> to say no to smoking. ( ) _____

2 His story was <u>good too</u> to be true. ( ) _____

3 Darryl went to France <u>in to order</u> learn French. ( ) _____

4 We sold lemonade <u>so as to</u> make some money. ( ) _____

5 She had no choice <u>but sell</u> her hair. ( ) _____

6 Drusilla was too foolish <u>believe</u> what he said. ( ) _____

7 <u>To begin with</u>, you need to get fit ( ) _____

C 다음 글의 밑줄 친 부분 중, 어법상 틀린 것은?

Did you know that MP3 was ① <u>invented</u> by a group of engineers from several different countries? They were from France, Germany, and the United States. They wanted to record sounds clearly and ② <u>make</u> recordings as small as possible. ③ <u>In order do this</u>, they needed to do two tasks. First, they needed to remove unimportant data. Second, they needed to keep important data. It took them several years ④ <u>to finish</u> the job. And thanks to them, we can now ⑤ <u>enjoy</u> clear and beautiful sound.

Form

1 We **had** the maintenance specialists **repair** our roof.
  We **felt** the cold water **splash** against our backs.

2 They **couldn't but feel** sorry for the little girl.
  They **couldn't help** feel**ing** sorry for the little girl.

3 James **does nothing but sleep**.

4 I **would rather die** than **eat** broccoli.

Meaning & Use

1_ to 없이 "동사 원형"의 형태로 쓰이는 부정사를 "원형부정사"라고 하는데, 앞서 살펴봤듯이, 사역동사나 지각동사의 목적격보어로 쓰인다.

The manager made the clerk clean the office.

I could hear the water drip down my neck.

2_ 원형부정사는 또한 여러 관용표현에 쓰이는데, 표현의 형태를 정확히 익혀두어야 한다. "cannot but 원형부정사(~)"는 "~하지 않을 수 없다"는 뜻으로 "cannot help -ing"로 바꾸어 나타낼 수 있다.

Buffy couldn't but forgive him for his honest mistake.

≒ Buffy couldn't help forgiving him for his honest mistake.

3_ "do nothing but 원형부정사(~)"는 "~하기만 하다"라는 뜻을 나타낸다. but 다음에 원형부정사가 와야 함에 특히 주의해야 한다.

Willow did nothing but cry.

4_ "would rather 원형부정사(~) than 원형부정사(…)"는 "…하느니 차라리 ~편이 낫다"라는 뜻을 나타낸다.

I would rather die than learn Japanese.

Key point_ 목적격 보어로서 원형부정사 **vs.** 과거분사

TEPS 등의 영어 시험에서는 사역동사나 지각동사의 목적격보어로 원형부정사가 와야 하는지, 과거분사가 와야 하는지를 자주 측정한다. 목적어가 목적격보어가 나타내는 행동을 하면 원형부정사를, 그렇지 않고 당하면 과거분사를 써야 한다고 정확히 익혀두어야 한다.

I had the doctor check my eyes. / I had my eyes checked by the doctor.

Exercises

A 적절한 것을 괄호 안에서 고르시오.

1 A few days ago, Jonathan had a strange thing (happen, happened) to him.

2 Can you make yourself (understand, understood) in Spanish?

3 The old lady had her daughter (injure, injured) in the accident.

4 We heard the song (play, played) by a famous singer.

5 They saw their only son (kick, kicked) their horse.

6 To my great surprise, I felt something (move, moved) inside of me.

7 I would rather die than (to read, read) The New York Times.

B 밑줄 친 부분이 어법에 맞으면 T, 맞지 않으면 F라고 쓰고 맞게 고치시오.

1 We had our faces <u>painted</u> red for the
football game. ( ) _____

2 The teacher made her students <u>studied</u>
much harder. ( ) _____

3 Sarah had her hair <u>to cut</u> at the salon. ( ) _____

4 Sandra heard her name <u>call</u> by someone. ( ) _____

5 Eric could feel his heart <u>beaten</u> faster. ( ) _____

6 Barbara did nothing but <u>to wait</u>. ( ) _____

7 I had my foot <u>stepped</u> on a few times by Fred. ( ) _____

C 다음 글의 밑줄 친 부분 중, 어법상 틀린 것은?

When I was a high school student, I tutored a boy in English. I ①went to his home three times a week. He was three years younger than me. Unlike other boys his age, he was very sensitive and thoughtful. As time went by, I came ②to like him. I tried ③to hide my feelings, but that was too difficult. When his parents ④found this out, they fired me. I was all in tears for several days. What hurt me most was that I couldn't see him anymore. These sad memories made me ⑤became a great romance novelist.

Chapter Review

A   잘못된 곳을 고치시오.

1   We want moving to the Netherlands.

2   They decided bought a new computer.

3   To our surprise, she refused help the police find the criminal.

4   They expected meeting the famous politician.

5   Brian had hoped built a large hotel.

6   My mother needs a shorter broom clean the kitchen floor.

7   There is an assistant helped you with your needs.

8   The students seemed to were nice.

9   As time went by, we came love the church.

10   The event was to be hold at City Hall.

11   I must wake up early caught the sunrise.

12   We were disappointed to hearing that the concert had been canceled.

13   His grandfather lived be eighty.

14   We washed our hands to got ready for dinner.

15   I'm here met Mr. Robinson.

16   Susan was careless too to look after her sister.

17   Erica was enough wise to avoid seeing the lazy young man.

18   The question was too difficult for anyone to solved.

19   In to order pass the test, you must study for years.

20   They had no choice but move to the United States.

21   I am having my teeth cleans at the dentist's office today.

22   The boss made the employees worked too hard.

23   He had his feet massage by a famous masseuse.

24   I would rather die than selling my own car.

25   Sarah did nothing but to sing.

B (A), (B), (C)의 각 괄호 안에서 어법에 맞는 표현을 골라 짝지은 것으로 가장 적절한 것은?

In my opinion, scuba diving is great for us. First of all, it gives us a chance to see a different world. We think we know a lot about our world, but we do not! By (A) [to go / going] to a very different place, we can learn a lot about both the place and our land. Second, scuba diving gives us a chance to become strong. Some people believe that it is very dangerous. But with the help of special devices, we can (B) [go / gone] to the underwater world safely. We can also learn how to do things underwater. This makes us strong. In short, scuba diving is a great way (C) [experience / to experience] our world and be strong.

	(A)	(B)	(C)
①	to go	gone	experience
②	going	go	experience
③	to go	gone	to experience
④	going	go	to experience
⑤	going	gone	experience

C 다음 글의 밑줄 친 부분 중, 어법상 틀린 것은?

In order to write well, you need ① to think clearly. This may sound very simple and easy, but it is not. In fact, you ought to think really hard ② written clear sentences. This is quite different from speech because you do not have to think clearly when ③ speaking. Since you have face-to-face conversation with other people, they can easily ④ understand what you are trying to say. But your readers have nothing but your writing in understanding what you are trying to say. So think and ⑤ express clearly.

Chapter Review

D 다음 밑줄 친 부분에 가장 적절한 것을 고르시오.

1 Stella chose _____ the team.
- a. join
- b. joins
- c. to join
- d. joining

2 Finally, they decided _____ up.
- a. give
- b. gave
- c. giving
- d. to give

3 Everybody wants _____ a star.
- a. be
- b. to be
- c. being
- d. is

4 They planned _____ him on the weekend.
- a. to visit
- b. visiting
- c. visit
- d. visits

5 The service was _____ performed on February 1.
- a. be
- b. to
- c. to be
- d. to being

6 Please give me time _____ about my decision.
- a. think
- b. to think
- c. thinking
- d. thought

7 Kevin seemed _____ her.
- a. to like
- b. to liking
- c. liking
- d. liked

8 We need some pencils to _____.
- a. write
- b. write with
- c. writing
- d. written

9 Can you come over tonight _____ dinner?
- a. eat
- b. eating
- c. eaten
- d. to eat

10 Everybody was _____ to hear that the hostages had been released.
- a. delighted
- b. delight
- c. delighting
- d. delights

11 Tom grew up _____ a brave soldier.

a. be

b. to be

c. was

d. to being

12 We were sad _____ the news.

a. hear

b. heard

c. to hear

d. to hearing

13 Ally was _____ to follow his sensible advice.

a. enough wise

b. enough foolish

c. foolish enough

d. wise enough

14 _____ get ready for school, they needed to prepare a lot of things.

a. To in order

b. In order to

c. In to order

d. To order in

15 They had no choice _____ their house.

a. but abandon

b. except abandon

c. but to abandon

d. abandoning

16 The child was so _____ catch the thief.

a. brave as

b. as brave to

c. to brave as

d. brave as to

17 We saw fish _____ in the lake.

a. swum

b. swim

c. to swim

d. swims

18 She had her only daughter _____ in the accident.

a. kill

b. killing

c. killed

d. kills

19 I would rather die than _____ grammar rules.

a. to memorize

b. memorizing

c. memorized

d. memorize

20 He had his car _____ last night.

a. steal

b. stolen

c. stealing

d. steals

Chapter 6

동명사

Form

1 **Playing** soccer inside the house can be dangerous.
I enjoy **watching** TV after I get home from school.
My hobby is **collecting** rare CDs.

2 Ethan was able to succeed by **working** hard.

3 We were used to **staying** up late at night.

4 Brooke **spent** so much time **playing** computer games.

Meaning & Use

1_ "동사원형＋ing"라는 형태로 명사 역할을 하는 어구를 동명사라고 한다. 명사처럼 문장에서 주어·목적어·보어의 역할을 맡을 수 있다. 현재분사도 "동사원형＋ing"라는 형태이지만 형용사 역할을 맡는다는 점에서 명사 역할을 하는 동명사와 다르다.

Eating too much ice cream is bad for your health. (동명사)

We miss going to the zoo. (동명사)

The hardest part of the job is controlling many types of people. (동명사)

Many children were attracted to the falling snow. (현재분사)

2_ 명사와 마찬가지로 동명사도 전치사의 목적어로 쓰일 수 있다. 대개 전치사의 목적어로는 to 부정사가 아니라 동명사가 온다는 점에 유의해야 한다.

There's no reason for fighting. (O) / There's no reason for to fight. (X)

3_ 다음 세 가지 표현은 정확히 구별해서 익혀두어야 한다.

> be used to 동명사(~) : ~하는 데 익숙하다
> be used to 동사원형(~): ~하기 위해 사용되다
> used to 동사원형(~): ~하곤 했다; ~였다

They were used to living in the country.

They were used to make drugs.

They used to play the drums.

4_ "spend＋시간＋동명사(~) [~하는 데 시간을 보내다]"는 중요한 표현으로 익혀두어야 한다.

She spent some time working with other volunteers.

Exercises

A 적절한 것을 괄호 안에서 고르시오.

1 (Watching, Watch) TV for too long is bad for your eyes.

2 I enjoy (to write, writing) about dragons.

3 The children were used to (live, living) on a farm.

4 These materials are used to (build, building) a bridge.

5 Alice (used to, was used to) spend time with me.

6 Cars are used for (driving, to drive).

7 Britney spent so much time (to practice, practicing).

B 밑줄 친 부분이 어법에 맞으면 T, 맞지 않으면 F라고 쓰고 맞게 고치시오.

1 Lucy enjoys <u>eating</u> apple pies. ( ) _____

2 You can achieve many things by <u>to work</u> hard. ( ) _____

3 She <u>was used</u> to be a nice person. ( ) _____

4 Those factories were used <u>to make</u> weapons. ( ) _____

5 I'm not used <u>to live</u> in America. ( ) _____

6 Thomas loves <u>relaxed</u> at the beach. ( ) _____

7 Isabella spent so much time <u>to watch</u> TV. ( ) _____

C 다음 글의 밑줄 친 부분 중, 어법상 틀린 것은?

Some people think that scuba diving ① is fun. I disagree. First of all, it is very dangerous. The underwater world is very different from our land. There is no air, and you can ② die there. Second, we can see the underwater world without ③ to go there. There ④ are lots of pictures and movies about it. So, just be safe and ⑤ do not think about scuba diving!

Form

1 **Learning** new things can be exciting.

2 Charlotte talked about **having visited** China.

3 How do you feel about **being required** to go through customs?

4 Dylan lied about **having been accepted** to medical school.

Meaning & Use

1_ 동명사는 동사의 특성을 유지하기 때문에 시제와 태를 나타낼 수 있다. 단순형은 [동사원형+ing]라는 본래 형태를 취한다.

Watching the movie will make you cry.

2_ 문장의 시제보다 더 이전을 나타내는 완료형 동명사는 [having+과거분사]라는 형태를 취한다. 목적어로 동명사만이 오는 동사 가운데 admit(시인하다), deny(부인하다), mention(언급하다) 다음에는 종종 완료형 동명사가 온다.

Brady lied about having started drinking.

Aaron admitted having killed the snake.

Gabriel denied having stolen the money.

Lily mentioned having visited over fifty countries.

3_ 일정한 동작을 하는 것이 아니라 당한다는 뜻을 나타내는 경우에는 [being+과거분사]라는 형태를 취한다.

Noah is the kind of person who helps others without being asked.

They enjoyed being entertained by clowns.

4_ 완료와 수동의 의미를 동시에 나타내는 경우에는 [having+been+과거분사]라는 형태를 취한다.

How did you feel about having been deceived by your best friend?

Exercises

A   적절한 것을 괄호 안에서 고르시오.

1   (Swam, Swimming) in the deep end is dangerous.

2   Sophia talked about (having, being) worked with the famous scientist.

3   Juliet admitted (having, being) dated Romeo.

4   Romeo denied (having, being) dated Juliet.

5   Liam mentioned (having, being) designed a building.

6   How did you feel about (having been, having) invited to the reception?

7   Evan admitted (having, being) robbed the bank.

B   밑줄 친 부분이 어법에 맞으면 T, 맞지 않으면 F라고 쓰고 맞게 고치시오.

1   <u>Chasing</u> cats was the dog's favorite hobby.   ( ) _____

2   Ava lied about <u>being</u> traveled to Canada.   ( ) _____

3   Alexander admitted <u>being</u> murdered the chef. ( ) _____

4   Emma denied <u>having damaged</u> the car.   ( ) _____

5   Brooke mentioned <u>being interviewed</u>
the President.   ( ) _____

6   Olivia admitted <u>having cheated</u> on
her husband.   ( ) _____

7   Jack denied <u>being cheated</u> on his wife.   ( ) _____

C   다음 글의 밑줄 친 부분 중, 어법상 틀린 것은?

I believe that ① <u>giving books</u> is much better for children. First of all, books
stay with us for a long time, but flowers don't. In fact, you can ② <u>have</u>
books all your life. They are like your best friends. Second, books teach
us a lot of things. You can learn everything from books. They also teach
us ③ <u>to think</u>. ④ <u>Being thought</u> makes you live a better and happier life.
So, giving books is a better idea than ⑤ <u>giving flowers</u>.

Unit 03 동명사 vs. 부정사

Form

> 1 I **enjoyed watching** cartoons on Saturday mornings.
>
> 2 In fact, Superman hates **flying**.
>   In fact, Superman hates **to fly**.
>
> 3 I remember **doing** my assignment.
>   I remembered **to do** my assignment.
>
> 4 Audrey stopped **smoking**.
>   Audrey stopped **to smoke**.

Meaning & Use

1_ 목적어로 동명사나 to부정사가 오는 동사는 다음 네 가지 종류로 나뉜다.

   i) 목적어로 동명사만이 오는 동사: admit, deny, enjoy, finish, mention, mind, stop

   ii) 목적어로 to부정사만이 오는 동사: choose, decide, expect, hope, plan, want 등

   iii) 둘 다 오면서 뜻이 같은 동사: begin, continue, hate, like, love, start

   iv) 둘 다 오면서 뜻이 다른 동사: forget, regret, remember, try

   Would you mind opening the door? (O) / Would you mind to open the door? (X)

2_ 1의 iii) 에서 제시한 동사들은 목적어로 to부정사가 오든 동명사가 오든 뜻의 차이가 거의 없다. 시작(begin, start)이나 계속(continue) 또는 선호 여부(like, love, hate)를 나타내는 동사들이 여기에 속한다.

   I loved reading books as a child. / I loved to read books as a child.

3_ 1의 iv)에서 제시한 동사들은 대개 to부정사가 오면 앞으로 할 일에 대해, 동명사가 오면 이미 일어난 일을 묻는 것이 보통이다. 다음 동사들은 이와 다른 경우이다.

   > regret ~ing: ~한 것을 후회하다   /   regret to ~ : 유감스럽게도 ~하다
   > try ~ing: 시험 삼아 ~해 보다   /   try to ~ : ~하려고 노력하다

   We regret to inform you that your application has been declined.
   We regretted having sent the application.

4_ stop 다음에 to부정사가 와서 "stop to ~"로 쓰이면 "~하기 위해서 (하던 일이나 가던 길을) 멈추다"라는 뜻이 된다.

   Logan stopped drinking. / Logan stopped to drink.

Exercises

A   적절한 것을 괄호 안에서 고르시오.

1   Claire admitted (to have, having) broken into her house.

2   James finished (to write, writing) an article.

3   They decided (to sell, selling) their boat.

4   We continued (watch, watching) the movie.

5   Sadly for us, our pet stopped (breathing, to breathe).

6   He regretted (to have, having) made such a stupid mistake.

7   Would you mind (to help, helping) me move the table?

B   밑줄 친 부분이 어법에 맞으면 T, 맞지 않으면 F라고 쓰고 맞게 고치시오.

1   I enjoyed <u>cooking</u> for the restaurant.   ( ) _____

2   They planned <u>building</u> a large bridge.   ( ) _____

3   We regret <u>telling</u> you that you failed the test. ( ) _____

4   The couple chose <u>staying</u> at the hotel.   ( ) _____

5   Liam admitted <u>to have</u> committed a crime.   ( ) _____

6   Caleb mentioned <u>to have</u> fought with him.   ( ) _____

7   Boyd denied <u>to have</u> broken the window.   ( ) _____

C   다음 글의 밑줄 친 부분 중, 어법상 틀린 것은?

Is a firefly a fly? No, it isn't. A fly has one pair of wings, but a firefly ① has two pairs of wings. Then what is it? A firefly is a beetle. Do you know that some fireflies do not eat at all? ② No, they don't. Isn't that ③ amazing? And why do fireflies make light? To help us find a place? To please us? A lot of scientists think their light is a warning against their predators. The light tells the predators that fireflies taste bad. So most predators do not try ④ to kill fireflies. But, sadly for us, frogs enjoy ⑤ to eat lots of fireflies.

Form

1 **It's no use** crying over spilt milk.

2 The film *D-War* **is worth** watch**ing**.

3 I feel **like** go**ing** out tonight.

4 **On** see**ing** the police officer, the robber ran away.
In writ**ing** an article about travel, be as specific as possible.

5 The country **was on the point of** declar**ing** war against Iraq.
I **make a point of** wak**ing** up early in the morning.

Meaning & Use

1_ 동명사는 여러 관용 표현에 활용된다. 그 가운데 It's no use ~ing는 "~해 봐야 소용없다"는 뜻을 나타낸다.
It's no use regretting the past.

2_ be worth ~ing는 "~할 만한 가치가 있다"는 뜻을 나타낸다.
Canada is worth visiting.

3_ feel like ~ing는 "~하고 싶은 생각이 들다"라는 뜻을 나타낸다.
They felt like visiting their grandparents.

4_ on ~ing는 "~하자마자"라는 뜻을, in ~ing는 "~할 때; ~함에 있어서"라는 뜻을 나타낸다.
on ~ing는 몇 가지 표현으로 바꾸어 나타낼 수 있다.
On entering the room, she burst into tears.
≒ As soon as she entered the room, she burst into tears.
≒ No sooner had she entered the room than she burst into tears.
≒ Scarcely had she entered the room when she burst into tears.
≒ She had scarcely entered the room when she burst into tears.
≒ Hardly had she entered the room when she burst into tears.

5_ be on the point of ~ing는 "막 ~하려고 하다"라는 뜻을, make a point of ~ing는 "~하는 것을 규칙으로 삼다"라는 뜻을 나타낸다.
She makes a point of visiting her mother every day.
≒ She makes it a rule to visit her mother every day.

Exercises

A   적절한 것을 괄호 안에서 고르시오.

1   It is no use (tells, telling) them that they should behave well.
2   Her latest novel is worth (reading, reading it).
3   She felt like (drinking, to drink) alone.
4   On (met, meeting) her nephew, she hugged him.
5   No sooner (have, had) they started working than it began snowing.
6   Scarcely had she seen him when he (begun, began) to run away.
7   She makes it a rule (to see, seeing) her son every day.

B   밑줄 친 부분이 어법에 맞으면 T, 맞지 않으면 F라고 쓰고 맞게 고치시오.

1   It is no use <u>arguing</u> with him.   ( ) _____

2   Scarcely <u>he had</u> closed his eyes when it began raining.   ( ) _____

3   No sooner <u>she had</u> opened the door than she shouted.   ( ) _____

4   Daniel felt like <u>drinking</u> a beer.   ( ) _____

5   Emily makes a point <u>of to go</u> to bed early.   ( ) _____

6   Germany was on the point of <u>attacked</u> France.   ( ) _____

7   In <u>to explore</u> this matter, you need to be cautious.   ( ) _____

C   다음 글의 밑줄 친 부분 중, 어법상 틀린 것은?

A recession forced a company ① <u>to fire</u> an employee. The employee happened ② <u>to be</u> a father who had a warm heart. He even lent a lot of money to a desperate friend of his who tried ③ <u>to deceive</u> him. The father decided ④ <u>to do</u> so because he knew his friend was in much deeper trouble than he was. And, with the help of his daughter and one of his neighbors, he succeeded in ⑤ <u>to regain</u> his self-confidence and making his family find happiness again.

Chapter Review

A   잘못된 곳을 고치시오.

1   Drink milk is something I do daily.

2   She was used to driven a big car.

3   The factories are used to making furniture.

4   They were used to be good friends.

5   Sundays are usually for to relax at home.

6   They spent so much time to make up a story.

7   Angie is really good at play the guitar.

8   They lied about being dealt with the matter appropriately.

9   Boyce admitted having been shot the innocent man.

10   Jacob denied being met his wife at the restaurant.

11   Noah mentioned having being traveled to New York.

12   The soldiers proceeded without having frightened by any fear.

13   Chloe admitted being broken the picture frame.

14   We did not enjoy to listen to the president's speech.

15   Would you mind to help me carry these boxes?

16   Ryan finished to write the report.

17   We regretted to make the terrible mistake.

18   As he felt tired, he stopped taking a rest.

19   Susan wanted becoming a famous musician.

20   Robert chose living in Japan.

21   It's no use tell them to be quiet.

22   The film E.T. is worth watching them.

23   Peter felt like to drink sake.

24   Hardly he had closed the window when it began raining.

25   Sarah makes a point of to do her homework before dinner.

B (A), (B), (C)의 각 괄호 안에서 어법에 맞는 표현을 골라 짝지은 것으로 가장 적절한 것은?

Do you know what the United Nations does for peace? You see, the international organization does a lot of things to bring and (A) [keep / keeping] peace in the world. In a sense, keeping peace is what the United Nations is all about. It persuades many countries to stop (B) [to make, making] weapons that kill a large number of people. The United Nations also does many peacekeeping activities in many parts of the world. Everyone in the world (C) [wish, wishes] that its efforts could make this world a better place for all.

	(A)	(B)	(C)
①	keeping	to make	wish
②	keep	to make	wish
③	keeping	making	wishes
④	keep	making	wishes
⑤	keep	making	wish

C 다음 글의 밑줄 친 부분 중, 어법상 틀린 것은?

Do you know ① who Annalise Blum is? She is a young woman from the U.S. After ② finishing high school and before entering college, she spent one year ③ to help others in foreign countries. At first, she just thought that she needed some rest. But later, she realized that the decision changed her life forever. In Guatemala, she ④ taught English to fifty-five students. In Thailand, she helped those who lost their homes. ⑤ By making friends with a lot of people, she realized the worth of togetherness. And she had fun!

D   다음 밑줄 친 부분에 가장 적절한 것을 고르시오.

1   _____ water from the fountain is not very safe.
   a. Drink   b. Drank
   c. To drinking   d. Drinking

2   The spoon is used for _____ food into the mouth.
   a. to scoop   b. scooped
   c. scooping   d. scoop

3   Tom is used to _____ in a big house.
   a. live   b. lives
   c. lived   d. living

4   Susie spends to much time _____ about small things.
   a. worry   b. worrying
   c. to worry   d. worries

5   I am more used to _____ chopsticks.
   a. use   b. for use
   c. using   d. uses

6   Sandra mentioned _____ visited Thailand.
   a. being   b. to be
   c. be   d. having

7   Jim lied about _____ met the client.
   a. being   b. having
   c. be   d. have

8   Greg denied _____ danced with Mary.
   a. have   b. to have
   c. having   d. had

9   Jason works hard without _____ told to do so.
   a. be   b. being
   c. to be   d. to have

10   Toby admitted _____ made a serious mistake.
   a. have   b. to have
   c. having   d. has

11 Everybody wants _____ rich.
   a. getting   b. get
   c. gotten   d. to get

12 Do you enjoy _____ magazines?
   a. to read   b. read
   c. reading   d. reads

13 Would you mind _____ the old lady cross the street?
   a. to help   b. helping
   c. help   d. helped

14 They planned _____ to Egypt.
   a. traveling   b. travel
   c. to travel   d. to traveling

15 All of us expected _____ the reception.
   a. attending   b. to attend
   c. attend   d. attends

16 It's no use _____ too much.
   a. expect   b. expected
   c. expects   d. expecting

17 Her poem is worth _____ .
   a. read   b. reading
   c. reads   d. to reading

18 They felt like _____ on strike.
   a. to go   b. go
   c. going   d. gone

19 Hardly _____ shut the door when someone shouted at her.
   a. she had   b. she having
   c. having she   d. had she

20 Mark makes it a rule _____ tennis every weekend.
   a. playing   b. to play
   c. play   d. played

Chapter 7

분사

분사의 형태와 쓰임새

Form

1 The soccer game excited all the club members.
The soccer game was **exciting**.
All the club members were **excited**.

2 Catch the **rolling** ball on the grass.

3 This novel is **written** in Japanese.

4 On a New Year's Day, we went to the beach to see the **rising** sun.

Meaning & Use

1_ 분사란 동사 원형에 -ing나 -ed를 붙여 동사를 형용사처럼 쓸 수 있게 변형한 것으로 현재분사와 과거분사로 나뉜다.

All the students were bored.

His lecture was so boring.

2_ 현재분사는 [동사원형＋ing]의 형태로 "~하는, ~하고 있는"의 뜻을 가진다. 능동이나 진행의 의미로 쓰인다.

Do you see the man working on the roof?

My brother is working hard on his report.

3_ 과거분사는 [동사원형＋ed]의 형태로 "~한, ~된"의 뜻을 가진다. 수동이나 완료의 의미로 쓰인다. (불규칙동사의 과거분사는 부록 참조)

The computer was fixed by my neighbor.

I haven't finished my homework yet.

4_ 분사는 형용사처럼 쓰여 명사를 수식하는데, 분사 혼자 쓰일 경우에는 명사 앞에서, 분사가 구를 이루어 쓰일 때는 명사 뒤에서 이를 수식한다.

I'd like to have grilled chicken for dinner.

I'd like to eat pizza topped with Italian sausage and fresh mushrooms.

5_ 분사는 주어나 목적어를 보충 설명하는 보어 역할을 한다. "~하면서, ~한 채로"의 뜻을 가진다.

Jessica smiled winking her eye. / We left the house unlocked.

Exercises

A   적절한 것을 괄호 안에서 고르시오.

1   She was (watching, watched) TV late at night.

2   My grandfather is (sleeping, slept) in his bedroom.

3   The mouse has (eating, eaten) its supper.

4   The sleeping dog was (awakening, awakened) by a loud noise.

5   Who are you (talking, talked) to right now?

6   Please fill out the (requiring, required) documents.

7   The (falling snow, snow fallen) covered everything in sight.

B   밑줄 친 부분이 어법에 맞으면 T, 맞지 않으면 F라고 쓰고 맞게 고치시오.

1   We are <u>swimming</u> in the swimming pool.   ( ) _____

2   We have <u>watching</u> the new *Harry Potter* movie.   ( ) _____

3   The <u>talked</u> parrot could say many words.   ( ) _____

4   The new album has not yet been <u>released</u>.   ( ) _____

5   My father is <u>cooked</u> in the kitchen.   ( ) _____

6   The <u>brightening</u> day began as the rooster crowed.   ( ) _____

7   <u>Run</u> trains stop at around midnight in the city.   ( ) _____

C   다음 글의 밑줄 친 부분 중, 어법상 틀린 것은?

When I first learned English as a child, I had great difficulty ① <u>understanding</u> how English works. I wondered, "What are all these ② <u>funny-looking</u> letters? What do these strange words mean, anyway? How should I put these words together ③ <u>to make</u> a sentence? And what is English? Why should I learn it?" As I continued ④ <u>to learn</u> English, I was able to find the answers to some of the questions. Still, the other questions remain ⑤ <u>unanswering</u>.

현재분사 vs. 동명사

Form

1 My sister is **washing** the dishes right now.

2 **Playing** computer games is a lot of fun.

3 The boys and girls are **baking** bread.

4 One of my favorite things is **reading** comic books with my son.

Meaning & Use

1_   현재분사는 "~하는, ~하고 있는"의 뜻이다. 문장에서 형용사 역할을 하며, 명사를 수식하거나 현재진행형 등에 쓰인다.

People were so annoyed by the barking dog. (명사 수식)

The soccer team is practicing for the final match. (현재진행형)

2_   동명사는 "~하기, ~하는 것"의 뜻으로 명사적 성질을 가지며, 문장에서 주어·목적어·보어 역할을 한다.

Eating apples can be good for you. (주어)

I enjoy watching documentary films. (동사의 목적어)

Thank you for inviting me for the ceremony. (전치사의 목적어)

My hobby is cooking Italian food. (보어)

3_   be 동사 다음에는 현재분사와 동명사가 모두 올 수 있기 때문에 쓰임에 유의해야 한다. 현재분사가 오면 진행형으로 쓰여 "~하고 있는 중이다"라는 의미를 나타낸다. 이때 현재분사가 이끄는 부분이 주어와 동일한 관계에 있지 않다는 점에 주의해야 한다.

My grandmother is walking her dogs now. (My grandmother ≠ walking)

The baby has been crying for an hour. (The baby ≠ crying)

4_   be 동사 다음에 동명사가 오면 보어로 쓰여 "~하는 것"이라는 뜻이 된다. 이때 동명사가 이끄는 부분이 주어와 동일한 관계에 있다는 점에 유의해야 한다.

My grandmother's hobby is walking her dogs on sunny days.

(My grandmother's hobby = walking)

Exercises

A 밑줄 친 부분이 동명사이면 "동", 현재분사이면 "분"이라고 쓰시오.

1 She is <u>studying</u> to be a doctor. _____

2 I am <u>running</u> away from the angry dogs. _____

3 He loves <u>eating</u> strawberries in the summer. _____

4 The <u>singing</u> children danced happily _____

5 He's <u>diving</u> into the water. _____

6 Derek's plan is <u>making</u> chocolate cake for his girlfriend. _____

7 <u>Rejoicing</u> on Christmas day is a tradition for many people. _____

B 밑줄 친 부분이 어법에 맞으면 T, 맞지 않으면 F라고 쓰고 맞게 고치시오.

1 Gerald is <u>plays</u> basketball in the gym. ( ) _____

2 <u>Listening</u> to rap music is his favorite past time. ( ) _____

3 <u>Play</u> tennis is very popular in this country. ( ) _____

4 I enjoy <u>watched</u> TV after eating dinner. ( ) _____

5 I hate <u>going</u> to the doctor's office. ( ) _____

6 I haven't <u>seeing</u> her at all today. ( ) _____

7 We <u>reading</u> the questions on the test. ( ) _____

C 다음 글의 밑줄 친 부분 중, 어법상 틀린 것은?

The teacher tells us about our ① <u>loving mothers</u>. Just like the passage, she thinks that our mothers are very ② <u>important</u> to us. First of all, they love us very much. So they look after us very well. They do a lot of things like cooking and ③ <u>to work</u>. Second, our mothers want us ④ <u>to be happy</u>. So when we are sad, they are sad, too. When we are happy, they are happy, too. In short, we live ⑤ <u>happily</u> with the help of our mothers.

Form

1 A heavy snow is **falling** outside right now.

2 She was so **embarrassed** at his remark.

3 You certainly made me **disappointed**.

Meaning & Use

1_ 현재분사는 능동의 의미로 "(~가) …하게 하는"이란 뜻으로 쓰이거나, 진행의 의미로 "~하고 있는, ~하는 중인"이란 뜻으로 쓰인다.

This is a satisfying result for us. ("우리를 만족시키는" 결과)

They're all preparing for the final exam. (그들 모두 "준비하는 중인")

2_ 과거분사는 수동의 의미로 "~당한, ~해진"이라는 뜻으로 쓰이거나, 완료의 의미로 "~를 완료한"이라는 뜻으로 쓰인다.

You look very surprised at the news. (소식에 "놀란")

I've completed the job. ("끝마친")

3_ 분사는 사람의 감정을 나타낼 때도 쓰인다. "~한 감정을 느끼는"이라는 수동의 뜻일 때는 과거분사를, "~한 감정을 유발하는"이라는 능동의 뜻일 때는 현재분사를 쓴다.

It was an amazing performance. (놀라움을 유발하는)

All the audience were amazed by their performance. (놀라움을 느끼는)

4_ 분사가 목적격보어로 쓰일 때, 목적어와 목적격 보어가 능동의 관계이면 현재분사를, 수동의 관계일 때는 과거분사를 쓸 수 있다.

Didn't you hear me calling you? (내가 너를 부름)

He didn't hear his name called. (그의 이름이 불림을 당함)

Key point_ 현재분사 vs. 과거분사

TEPS 등의 어학시험에는 감정의 유발을 나타내는 현재분사가 사람과도 어울릴 수 있다는 점을 종종 출제한다. 그 사람이 일정한 감정을 유발하면 현재분사를 쓴다.

The professor is a very boring person. (지루함을 유발하는 사람)

Exercises

A 적절한 것을 괄호 안에서 고르시오.

1 Sarah has (talking, talked) to Sam.

2 We are (complaining, complained) about the lack of service.

3 Lisa doesn't want to buy a (using, used) computer.

4 The (barking, barked) dog isn't mine.

5 She had her (breaking, broken) bike fixed.

6 Do you know the girl (standing, stood) in front of the door?

7 I saw the guy (stealing, stolen) the wallet the other day.

B 밑줄 친 부분이 어법에 맞으면 T, 맞지 않으면 F라고 쓰고 맞게 고치시오.

1 Nobody noticed him <u>gone</u> out of the room.　(　) _____

2 The kids were <u>exciting</u> to go to the amusement park.　(　) _____

3 She made her gift box <u>wrapping</u> in a yellow paper.　(　) _____

4 People were <u>shocking</u> to see the car crashing.　(　) _____

5 I'm not <u>interested</u> in joining the club.　(　) _____

6 He is <u>watched</u> a movie on TV.　(　) _____

7 Have you <u>completed</u> the experiment?　(　) _____

C 다음 글의 밑줄 친 부분 중, 어법상 틀린 것은?

①In order to answer Type I questions, you need to have ②detailing information about the lectures. Thus, when listening, you ought ③to take notes. Of course, you do not have to write everything down. You will not have enough time ④to do that. You should, however, note down important examples or details. This is because you need those facts when ⑤composing your response.

분사구문의 형태와 쓰임새

Form

1 **Losing** my umbrella, I had to buy a new one.
Because I lost my umbrella, I had to buy a new one.

2 **Not knowing** the meaning, I said, "Yes."
Even though I didn't know the meaning, I said, "Yes."

3 **Frankly speaking**, he is not my boyfriend.

Meaning & Use

1_ 분사구문이란 분사를 이용하여 [접속사＋주어＋동사] 형태의 부사절을 간단하게 줄인 것을 말한다.

If you turn left, you'll see the French restaurant.

→ Turning left, you'll see the French restaurant.

2_ 분사구문은 다음과 같은 순서로 만든다.

■ 부사절의 접속사를 생략한다. (의미가 혼동될 수 있을 때는 접속사를 그대로 둔다.)

■ 부사절과 주절의 주어가 같으면 생략하고 다르면 그대로 둔다.

■ 부사절의 동사를 현재분사 형태로 바꾼다.

~~Because he~~ was hungry, he couldn't even stand.

→ (Being) Hungry, he couldn't even stand. (분사구문의 being은 생략 가능)

~~As she~~ didn't study enough, she couldn't get good marks.

→ Not studying enough, she couldn't get good marks. (부정어는 분사 앞에 위치)

3_ 분사구문은 시간(~할 때, ~하는 동안), 부대상황(~하면서 동시에), 원인(~이므로), 조건(만약 ~라면), 양보(~이지만, ~이더라도) 등의 뜻을 나타낸다.

Finishing her writing, she went out for dinner. (시간)

Washing the dishes, Roy kept talking to his daughter. (부대상황)

Feeling so tired, she went to bed earlier than usual. (원인)

Exercises

A 적절한 것을 괄호 안에서 고르시오.

1 Stretching its legs, the cat yawned quietly.

→ (If, While) it was stretching its legs, the cat yawned quietly.

2 Eating out every day, Thomas began to run out of money.

→ (As, When) he ate out every day, Thomas began to run out of money.

3 Living in Arizona, Sam hardly ever sees snow.

→ (While, Because) he lives in Arizona, Sam hardly ever sees snow.

4 Riding her bicycle, Sarah sang happily.

→ (Even though, While) she was riding her bicycle, Sarah sang happily.

B 밑줄 친 부분을 분사구문으로 바꿔 쓰시오.

1 <u>As soon as he took off his jacket</u>, Tony went out to play.

→ ＿＿＿＿＿＿＿＿＿＿＿＿＿＿＿＿＿＿, Tony went out to play.

2 <u>Even though he had not finished it</u>, he decided it was time for lunch.

→ ＿＿＿＿＿＿＿＿＿＿＿＿＿＿＿＿＿＿, he decided it was time for lunch.

3 <u>Because she was so scared</u>, Carol called 911.

→ ＿＿＿＿＿＿＿＿＿＿＿＿＿＿＿＿＿＿, Carol called 911.

4 <u>After he checked his email</u>, he was taken aback.

→ ＿＿＿＿＿＿＿＿＿＿＿＿＿＿＿＿＿＿, he was taken aback.

C 다음 글의 밑줄 친 부분 중, 어법상 틀린 것은?

I believe basketball is better for children. First of all, children need ①<u>to learn</u> to play together. In many cases, two people play badminton. When ②<u>played</u> basketball, however, you play with at least four other people on your team. So you will learn how ③<u>to play</u> as a team. Second, when you ④<u>play</u> basketball, you move your body much more. You need to run. You need to think and ⑤<u>move</u> quickly. In short, basketball teaches you more things than badminton.

Chapter Review

A   잘못된 곳을 고치시오.

1   The girl wore a blue cap is my niece.

2   We were surprising at her sudden death.

3   The movie was so bored.

4   I feel like to seeing an excited movie tonight.

5   Jerry has been played computer games for three hours.

6   People saw the building burning down by the big fire.

7   David is played the guitar in his room.

8   The letter was writing in Hebrew, so no one couldn't read it.

9   Jack wanted his house painting in blue.

10   Why do you look so worrying?

11   All the results were disappointed to me.

12   Could you please fix this desk broken?

13   It seems very interested to me.

14   The old woman lived next door is very kind.

15   Have you ever being to Canada?

16   The boss was not very satisfying with the result.

17   My father is read a newspaper in the living room now.

18   The tourist stood looked at the sign.

19   Everybody agreed that the concert was amazed.

20   The detective saw him stolen the bike.

21   Walk down the street, Lucy met her old friend.

22   Seen him, she run away.

23   She losing her book, she asked me to borrow mine.

24   If finding a wallet, Carl decided to take it to the police.

25   Knowing not what to say, he just kept silence.

B (A), (B), (C)의 각 괄호 안에서 어법에 맞는 표현을 골라 짝지은 것으로 가장 적절한 것은?

 Global warming is a serious problem that we have to deal with. If the world temperature (A) [will go / goes] up, glaciers will melt and drown many cities. In addition, hurricanes will become stronger because of more heat at sea. Moreover, some diseases (B) [carried / carrying] by mosquitoes will become worse and kill more people. Warmer weather will kill many different plants and animals that are (C) [using / used] to mild weather, too. In these ways, global warming is really bad for the earth.

	(A)	(B)	(C)
①	will go	carried	used
②	will go	carrying	using
③	goes	carried	used
④	goes	carrying	using
⑤	goes	carried	using

C 다음 글의 밑줄 친 부분 중, 어법상 틀린 것은?

I don't understand why some people commit fouls in soccer matches. Perhaps they think that it is O.K. ① to win a game by any means. Or they may think that people will be ② impressing by such "tough" play. In any case, they seem to believe that ③ winning is the most important goal of soccer matches. I disagree. Doing one's best and ④ accepting the consequences are much, much more important than winning in any sport. In fact, that is what sports are all about: ⑤ growing up as a true human being.

Chapter Review

다음 밑줄 친 부분에 가장 적절한 것을 고르시오.

1 The boss found him _____ at his desk.
a. sleep
b. sleeps
c. sleeping
d. has slept

2 I have been _____ English for three years.
a. study
b. studied
c. studying
d. to study

3 These pictures were _____ by Jessica.
a. take
b. taking
c. taken
d. for taking

4 I haven't _____ better soup anywhere else.
a. taste
b. tasted
c. tasting
d. been tasted

5 The old man _____ on the bench is Kevin's grandfather.
a. sit
b. sat
c. sitting
d. to sit

6 She couldn't sleep because she was so _____ about the result.
a. worry
b. worrying
c. worried
d. to worry

7 _____ out of the window, she sighed.
a. Look
b. Looks
c. Looking
d. Looked

8 My brother wants to have a PMP _____ in Japan.
a. make
b. to make
c. making
d. made

9 I heard his name _____ several times in the lecture.
a. mention
b. mentioned
c. mentioning
d. has mentioned

10 _____ the woman coming to the house, he went upstairs.
a. Know
b. Knowing
c. When he knew
d. As he knowing

118 | TOP GRAMMAR

11 They were surprised at the _____ .
   a. shock news   b. shocking news
   c. news shocked   d. news shocking

12 I've never heard him _____ ill of others.
   a. speaks   b. spoken
   c. speaking   d. for speaking

13 The big boy made his friend _____ his bag.
   a. carry   b. carried
   c. to carry   d. carries

14 The governor will be _____ the winners of the award soon.
   a. announce   b. announcing
   c. announced   d. being announced

15 The lecturer was _____ at the unexpected question from the audience.
   a. confuse   b. confusing
   c. confused   d. being confused

16 _____ by his grandchildren, he read a storybook to them.
   a. Surrounded   b. Surrounding
   c. Be surrounding   d. Being surround

17 _____ to play the piano, Fred began to love music.
   a. Learn   b. To learn
   c. Learning   d. Being learned

18 _____ the first train, he could get the meeting in time.
   a. Miss   b. Missing
   c. Not missing   d. Not missed

19 _____ by the fireplace, Lisa ate boxes and boxes of chocolate cookies.
   a. Sit   b. To sit
   c. Sitting   d. Sat

20 _____ rainy and windy, we stayed at home.
   a. Being   b. It being
   c. Having been   d. It been

Chapter 8

가정법

Form

1 If the weather **were** nice, I **would** play basketball.

2 If I **had been** there, I **would have** help**ed** you.

3 We **suggest** that you **listen** to the teacher's lectures.

Meaning & Use

1_ 가정법은 이루어지지 않았거나 이룰 수 없는 일에 대한 안타까움을 드러내는 표현 형태이다. 사실 관계만을 기준으로 할 때는 직설법으로 전환이 가능하지만, 직설법에는 말하는 이의 감정이 들어 있지 않다는 점에 유의해야 한다.

If it were snowing, I could build a snowman.

→ As it is not snowing, I cannot build a snowman.

2_ 가정법은 크게 가정법 과거와 가정법 과거완료로 나뉘는데, "과거"나 "과거완료"라는 표현은 if절이나 주절 동사의 형태를 가리킨다. 대개 실제와 한 시제가 차이가 나는 것이 보통이다.

If the sun were out, I would fly a kite. (가정법 과거: 현재 사실)

If you had tasted it, you could have liked it. (가정법 과거완료: 과거 사실)

3_ 일부 문법서에서는 "가정법 현재"를 설정하여 명령·제안·요구·주장을 나타내는 order, command (명령)/ suggest, propose (제안)/ ask, demand (요구)/ insist (주장)와 같은 동사 다음에 가정법 현재가 쓰인다고 설명하는데, 현대 영어에서는 일반적으로 가정법 현재를 설정하지 않는다. 본래 영국식 영어에서는 이런 동사 다음의 that절에 [should+동사원형]을 쓰지만 미국식 영어에서는 should를 생략하고 동사원형만 쓴다.

I demand that he take off his shoes before entering our house.

Key point _ insist/suggest 다음의 that절

수능 등의 시험에서는 제안과 주장을 나타내는 suggest와 insist 다음의 that절에 동사원형이나 과거형이 올 수 있음을 종종 측정한다. suggest가 "~해야 한다고 제안하다"일 때는 동사원형이, "~라고 시사하다"일 때는 시제일치에 따라 여러 시제가 온다. insist도 "~해야 한다고 주장하다"일 때는 동사원형이, "~라는 사실을 주장하다"일 때는 시제일치에 따라 여러 시제가 온다.

He insisted that we be quiet. / He insisted that we had made a mistake.

Exercises

A 적절한 것을 괄호 안에서 고르시오.

1 If she (was, were) here, I would give her a hug.

2 If you (are, were) kinder to others, you would be more popular.

3 If Billy (had, has) seen the movie, he would have liked it.

4 If he (have, had) given Sarah a birthday gift, she would have been delighted.

5 We demanded that they (had left, leave) our house.

6 He suggested that we (go, went) to the doctor's office.

7 I insist that you not (wait, waited) for me.

B 밑줄 친 부분이 어법에 맞으면 T, 맞지 않으면 F라고 쓰고 맞게 고치시오.

1 If there <u>were</u> no homework to do, I would play. ( ) _____

2 If I <u>have seen</u> you, I would have hugged you. ( ) _____

3 We suggest that everyone <u>be</u> present at this meeting.   ( ) _____

4 I demand that the seller <u>sent</u> me a refund.   ( ) _____

5 I insist you <u>was</u> polite your grandfather.   ( ) _____

6 I suggest you <u>take</u> your medicine.   ( ) _____

7 We demand you <u>had told</u> us the truth!   ( ) _____

C 다음 글의 밑줄 친 부분 중, 어법상 틀린 것은?

When my mother was a kid, her family was very poor. And her father didn't want her ① to attend school. Instead, he wanted her to work at a factory! But, always a keen student, she insisted that they ② sent her to school, and she became the first member of her family ③ to graduate from university. After graduation, she began ④ to work for an international company. And she believed that some day she ⑤ would become the president of a company. At last, her dream came true. After all, all her hard work paid off.

Form

> 1 **If** it **didn't snow** now, we **would play** soccer.
>
> 2 **If** you **didn't watch** so much TV, you **could study** harder.
>
> 3 **If** I **moved** to America, I **would live** in Beverly Hills.

Meaning & Use

1_ 가정법 과거는 현재 사실과 다르거나 앞으로 일어날 것 같지 않은 일을 나타낼 때 쓰인다. "~ 하다면 …할 텐데" 라는 뜻을 갖는다.

If I had a car, I would drive her home.

If I won the lottery, I would give all the money to you.

2_ 가정법 과거는 [If+주어+동사의 과거형, 주어+would/should/could/might+동사원형] 의 형태로 쓴다. be동사는 반드시 were를 써야 함에 유의해야 한다. 현재 사실에 반대되는 일을 나타내므로 직설법 현재로 바꾸어 표현할 수 있다.

If I were not sick, I would come with you.

→ As I'm sick, I won't come with you.

3_ 가정법 과거는 실현가능성이 희박한 현재 또는 미래의 일을 가정할 때도 쓰인다.

If I were a magician, I could change this into gold.

→ As I am not a magician, I can't change this into gold.

Key point_ should / were to 가정법

TEPS 등의 시험에서는 실현 가능성이 별로 없는 미래의 일을 나타낼 때 If절에 should나 were to를 쓴다는 것을 종종 출제한다. should나 were가 과거형이라는 점에 유의하자.

If anything should happen to me, give this note to Ms. Johnson.

If I were to meet my favorite singer, I would first shake his hands.

Exercises

A 적절한 것을 괄호 안에서 고르시오.

1 If it (is, were) Saturday, I could sleep late.

2 If I were at home, I (can, could) play video games all afternoon.

3 If Sam (was, were) my brother, we'd play basketball together every day.

4 If I (play, played) football, I would exercise more.

5 If you (drive, drove) faster, we'd get there on time.

6 If you (are to, were to) come over today, I would cook dinner for you.

7 If we (don't, didn't) go to church today, I would sleep in.

B 밑줄 친 부분이 어법에 맞으면 T, 맞지 않으면 F라고 쓰고 맞게 고치시오.

1 I <u>bought</u> you dinner if you were my teacher. ( ) ＿＿＿＿＿＿＿＿＿

2 If I <u>wasn't have</u> so much homework, I would play. ( ) ＿＿＿＿＿＿＿＿＿

3 If I <u>join</u> the class, I would try my best to get an A. ( ) ＿＿＿＿＿＿＿＿＿

4 I <u>will buy</u> everyone pizza if we should win the game. ( ) ＿＿＿＿＿＿＿＿＿

5 If it were raining, I <u>will</u> stay inside all day. ( ) ＿＿＿＿＿＿＿＿＿

6 Would you help me mow the lawn if I <u>am</u> to pay you? ( ) ＿＿＿＿＿＿＿＿＿

7 If I should win this match, I <u>will</u> buy drinks for everyone. ( ) ＿＿＿＿＿＿＿＿＿

C 다음 글의 밑줄 친 부분 중, 어법상 틀린 것은?

Have you ① <u>read</u> the novel *Frankenstein*? It is a novel ② <u>written</u> by Mary Shelley. You may think that this story is just about a monster. But you need to ③ <u>know</u> that the story was written during the days of the Industrial Revolution. In fact, this novel clearly shows us that the power of machines can be very dangerous. In addition, we need to be very cautious about ④ <u>developing</u> technology. If we ⑤ <u>to develop</u> dangerous technology, it could destroy us. Can you get the message of this amazing novel?

가정법 과거완료

Form

1 **If** you **had arrived** there in time, you **could have met** her.

2 **If** I **hadn't lost** her number, I **would have called** her right away.

3 **If** I **had studied** harder, I would have passed the test.
   → **Had I studied** harder, I would have passed the test.

Meaning & Use

1_ 가정법 과거완료는 과거 사실과 반대되는 일이나, 과거에 이루지 못한 일을 가정하는 데
쓰인다. "~했다면 …했을 텐데"라는 뜻이다.

If the wind hadn't been so strong, the bridge would not have collapsed.

If you had gone to the dentist, you would not have suffered from toothache.

2_ 가정법 과거완료는 [If+주어+had+과거분사, 주어+would/should/could/might+
have+과거분사]의 형태로 쓴다. 직설법 과거 문장으로 바꾸어 쓸 수 있다.

If I hadn't taken the train, I could not have met her.

→ As I took the train, I could met her.

(실제로는 기차를 탔다. 기차를 타지 못했다면 그녀를 만나지 못했을 것이라고 가정하는 것이다.)

If you had told him the truth, he would have forgiven you.

→ As you didn't tell him the truth, he didn't forgive you.

(실제로는 진실을 말하지 않았다. 진실을 말했다면 그가 용서했을 것이라고 가정하는 것이다.)

3_ If절에서 If를 생략하고 had를 문두로 내보내는 도치 형태로도 쓸 수 있다.

If we had had enough money, we could have gone to the baseball game.

→ Had we had enough money, we could have gone to the baseball game.

If you had come to my restaurant, I could have given you free food.

→ Had you come to my restaurant, I could have given you free food.

Exercises

A 적절한 것을 괄호 안에서 고르시오.

1 If you (have practiced, had practiced) harder, you would have won the game.

2 If you (asked, had asked) her, she would have come with you.

3 If we (woke up, had woken up) late, we would have missed the bus.

4 If Sam (had driven, hadn't driven) slowly, we could have been in an accident.

5 If you had made dinner, our guests (would love, would have loved) it.

6 If Sarah had told me about the problem, I could (had, have) helped her.

7 (Had, If had) you been here, I would have told you.

B 밑줄 친 부분이 어법에 맞으면 T, 맞지 않으면 F라고 쓰고 맞게 고치시오.

1 I would pay you if you <u>had helped</u>. ( ) _____

2 If we <u>went</u> together, you would not have been so lonely. ( ) _____

3 He would have asked you if you <u>have been</u> there. ( ) _____

4 If you didn't go to bed so late, you <u>would catch</u> the bus. ( ) _____

5 He would have been angry if you <u>had come</u> home late. ( ) _____

6 If I <u>had worked</u> harder, I would have made more money. ( ) _____

7 If you had not forgotten the key, we <u>could open</u> it. ( ) _____

C 다음 글의 밑줄 친 부분 중, 어법상 틀린 것은?

Sometimes I couldn't help ①smelling car exhaust, and it smelled ②terrible. When I smelled it, I also felt dizzy. What would ③had happened if this gas had filled the air? The problem was that car exhaust was filling our air. So, our air was getting dirty. And if that continued, we would have difficulty ④breathing. Our health would get worse, too. I believed it was time ⑤to use cars less and keep the air clean. In fact, there were a lot of ways to use cars less.

Unit 04 — as if / I wish

Form

1 I **wish** I **knew** what the future will be.

2 The girl trembled **as if** she **saw** a ghost.

3 **It's time** that you **took** this pill.

Meaning & Use

1_ 현재 이루기 어려운 소망이나 과거의 일에 대한 아쉬움을 나타낼 때 [주어＋wish＋가정법 과거/과거완료] 구문을 쓴다. "~라면 좋을/좋았을 텐데"라는 뜻이다.

I wish I were an actress. (현재 사실에 반대)

→ I'm sorry I'm not an actress.

I wish I hadn't hurt my arm. (과거 사실에 반대)

→ I'm sorry I hurt my arm.

2_ as if를 써서 현재 또는 과거의 사실과 반대되는 내용을 가정해서 말할 수 있다. [as if＋가정법 과거/과거완료]의 형태로 "마치 ~인/였던 것처럼"으로 해석할 수 있다.

He tells me as if he were a famous journalist. (현재 사실에 반대)

→ In fact, he isn't a famous journalist.

She acted as if she had never met him before. (과거 사실에 반대)

→ In fact, she met him before.

3_ 가정법[It's (high / about) time＋주어＋가정법 과거]라는 형태로 "(정말) ~해야 할 시간이 다"는 뜻을 나타낸다. 해야 할 일을 하지 않고 있다는 뜻에서 불평 또는 나무랄 때 사용된다. 가정법 과거 대신 should나 to부정사를 써서 나타낼 수도 있다.

It's time they arrived in London.

→ It's time they should arrive in London.

It's high [about] time you woke up.

→ It's high [about] time to wake up.

Exercises

A 적절한 것을 괄호 안에서 고르시오.

1. I wish my mom (were, had been) here with me now.
2. I wish I (went, had gone) to the concert last night.
3. I wish I (bought, had bought) the magazine then.
4. He talks as if he (were, had been) once a millionaire.
5. She talks as if she (visited, had visited) Europe several times before.
6. It's high time you (go, went) to school.
7. It's about time we (have, had) lunch. It's over two thirty.

B 밑줄 친 부분이 어법에 맞으면 T, 맞지 않으면 F라고 쓰고 맞게 고치시오.

1. I wish I <u>haven't said</u> that to her.　( ) ＿＿＿＿＿＿＿＿
2. I really miss my friend Simon. I wish he <u>were</u> here.　( ) ＿＿＿＿＿＿＿＿
3. I wish I <u>were</u> prettier.　( ) ＿＿＿＿＿＿＿＿
4. My bike is so old. I wish I <u>have</u> a new one.　( ) ＿＿＿＿＿＿＿＿
5. David talks as if he <u>will be</u> sick.　( ) ＿＿＿＿＿＿＿＿
6. She acts as if she <u>knows</u> everything. But she doesn't.　( ) ＿＿＿＿＿＿＿＿
7. The kid acted as if he <u>were</u> a grown-up.　( ) ＿＿＿＿＿＿＿＿

C 다음 글의 밑줄 친 부분 중, 어법상 틀린 것은?

Michael Jordan once said, "Some people want it ① to happen, some wish it ② will happen, others make it happen." What kind of person do you think Michael is? Yes, you're right. He is one of those who ③ make it happen. He was not a successful basketball player from the beginning. In fact, he was kicked out of his school basketball team because he was not tall enough. But he grew a little and ④ came back to his team. Since then, he had tried really hard to excel. He practiced ⑤ playing basketball every morning. As a result of this hard training, he was able to become one of the greatest basketball players in history.

Chapter Review

A   잘못된 곳을 고치시오.

1   We ask that he not went there.

2   He suggested that we will watch the new movie about World War II.

3   I demand that she called me in two hours.

4   We proposed that the country passed new laws about education.

5   I order that you are here on time.

6   If I study harder, I would get an A on this test.

7   If it was still morning, I could get breakfast at McDonald's.

8   We will know the material if we listened in class.

9   If I am taller, I would be a pro volleyball player.

10   If she were richer, she can buy that expensive house.

11   If Billy had ate his vegetables, he would have grown taller.

12   If you brought rice, I would have made Chinese food.

13   If we had gone to the meeting, we will have been disappointed.

14   If you did not eaten so much, you would not have been so sick.

15   We would have seen him if we went earlier.

16   We would have been wet if we had brought our umbrellas.

17   I would help you if you had asked me then.

18   I wish I didn't spend so much money yesterday.

19   I would call the police if I was Jenny.

20   If I could buy anything, I will buy the red car.

21   It's about time that you start for the train station.

22   Deborah talks as if she was my best friend.

23   Josh acted as if he will be a veteran in this field.

24   Had I had a DVD player, I would watch my favorite movies every day.

25   If you left your scarf at home, you would have been very cold.

B (A), (B), (C)의 각 괄호 안에서 어법에 맞는 표현을 골라 짝지은 것으로 가장 적절한 것은?

Today's students have a lot of things to do every day. Thus they seem (A) [to have / having] little time to read great poems. This is a loss not only to them, but also to us. It is because poems enable us to turn bad feelings into good ones. If people (B) [will / did] not read poems anymore, they would have bad feelings. Then it would be very difficult for people to get along with each other. You may think that (C) [listening / listen] to soft songs is the same as reading poems. But they are quite different. Poems give us deeper meanings than songs.

	(A)	(B)	(C)
①	having	will	listen
②	having	did	listen
③	to have	did	listening
④	to have	will	listen
⑤	to have	did	listen

C 다음 글의 밑줄 친 부분 중, 어법상 틀린 것은?

I want ① to have a really small notebook computer. I do not mean that I want to get a PDA. PDAs are too small, you know. Actually, I have great difficulty ② using them. So I want a notebook computer which ③ is half the size of today's notebook computer. If I ④ have such a computer, I would take it everywhere and enjoy all the latest features. ⑤ How convenient that would be!

D   다음 밑줄 친 부분에 가장 적절한 것을 고르시오.

1   If he _____ Superman, he could save the world.
     a. is   b. was
     c. were   d. be

2   I would drive everywhere in the city if I _____ a car.
     a. have   b. had
     c. will have   d. had have

3   If they _____ more, they would be a lot better at this sport.
     a. practice   b. practiced
     c. have practiced   d. would practiced

4   The clothes _____ wet if you had left them outside.
     a. got   b. had gotten
     c. will be gotten   d. would have gotten

5   If the dog _____ chased the cat, it would not have been attacked.
     a. would   b. has
     c. would not   d. had not

6   I would have bought you lunch _____ you had gone with me.
     a. if   b. as
     c. when   d. as if

7   _____ the teacher had taught better, I would have paid more
     attention.
     a. As   b. If
     c. As if   d. Had he

8   If you _____ your day watching cartoons, you would have done
     your homework.
     a. spent   b. didn't spend
     c. had not spent   d. would not spend

9   If the game _____ longer, I would have missed dinner.
     a. last   b. lasted
     c. will last   d. had lasted

10   It's time the concert _____.
     a. begins   b. began
     c. have begun   d. will begin

11 It's about time Toby _____ the project.
a. finishes   b. finished
c. would finish   d. had been finished

12 I wish it _____ rain.
a. be   b. is
c. will   d. would

13 I wish I _____ him more often. He must have been so lonely.
a. visit   b. visited
c. would visit   d. would have visited

14 Jefferson always talks as if he _____ something. But he's not.
a. knows   b. knew
c. has known   d. would have known

15 Susie _____ as if she were the boss in the team.
a. acting   b. acted
c. talk   d. talking

16 If it were warmer, the flowers _____.
a. blossom   b. will blossom
c. would blossom   d. had blossom

17 It is so cold. I wish I _____ my jacket.
a. bring   b. bringing
c. had brought   d. will bring

18 Had I an umbrella, I _____ you home.
a. walk   b. walked
c. could walk   d. would have walked

19 If Margo had lost her wallet, she _____.
a. cry   b. will cry
c. would cry   d. would have cried

20 If Tim _____ the boss, he would have been fired.
a. angry   b. angered
c. had angered   d. would have angered

Chapter 9

일치와 화법

Unit 01 수의 일치

Form

1 **Both** he **and** his brother *like* to play soccer.

2 **Either** Peter **or** I *am* to blame.

3 **Those bags** that he's showing to her *are* all handmade.

4 At least **two weeks** *is* required to review the whole materials.

5 **One** of us *is* responsible for the result.

Meaning & Use

1_ 주어가 단수이면 동사도 단수, 주어가 복수이면 동사도 복수인 것이 원칙이다. 두 개 이상의 주어가 and로 묶이면 동사는 복수형을 취한다. 단, each나 every 다음에 and로 연결된 주어가 오더라도 동사는 단수형을 취한다.
Every boy and girl *is* special.

2_ neither A nor B, either A or B, not only A but (also) B 다음에 오는 동사는 B에 수를 일치시킨다. not only A but also B는 B as well A로 바꾸어 나타낼 수 있는데, B as well as A의 경우에도 동사의 수를 B에 일치시켜야 한다.
Neither my sister nor *my parents like* raw fish.
Neither my parents nor *my sister likes* raw fish.

3_ 주어를 꾸며주는 수식어구는 동사의 수를 결정하는 데 영향을 미치지 않는다.
This book *about mammals is* very interesting.

4_ 시간, 거리, 금액은 하나의 단위로 생각할 때 단수 취급한다.
Two hours *is* enough to finish those things.
Ten dollars *is* all I have now.

5_ 전체 중 일부를 나타내는 A [half/ some/ most/ 분수] of B의 형태에서는 동사의 수는 of 다음의 명사의 수에 따라 정해진다. 또한, "a number of＋복수 명사"는 복수로, "the number of＋복수 명사"는 단수로 생각한다.
Some of them *have* to participate in the course.
Some of the work *is* tough but worthwhile for us.
The number of students in my class *is* 34.
A number of students *were* late for school.

Exercises

A   적절한 것을 괄호 안에서 고르시오.

1   The mayor and his friend (plays, play) golf.

2   James and Bob (is, are) talking on the phone.

3   Both he and his wife (is, are) on a business trip.

4   Thirty minutes (is, are) not very long for a presentation.

5   Neither the boss nor his secretary (understands, understand) her English.

6   Almost half of the apples in the box (is, are) rotten.

7   The flowers on the desk (is, are) from Stephen.

B   밑줄 친 부분이 어법에 맞으면 T, 맞지 않으면 F라고 쓰고 맞게 고치시오.

1   One of the boys <u>are</u> missing.   (   ) _____

2   Mary as well as her sisters <u>is</u> going abroad
    to study.   (   ) _____

3   Either my brothers or I <u>was</u> wrong.   (   ) _____

4   Most of the students <u>have</u> agreed to do that. (   ) _____

5   Most of his books <u>is</u> about space and
    technology.   (   ) _____

6   The number of new born babies <u>are</u>
    decreasing.   (   ) _____

7   A number of teachers <u>were</u> angry.   (   ) _____

C   다음 글의 밑줄 친 부분 중, 어법상 틀린 것은?

I believe that art classes are better for students than science classes. First of all, art classes give us a chance to show our feelings, which ① is very important in this busy world. We need to show our feelings ② to live a healthy life. Science classes do not allow us ③ to do that. Next, art classes are for everyone, but science classes are not. Science classes are for students who ④ want to be scientists. Not everybody ⑤ want to be a scientist. But everyone should learn how to express themselves. That is what art classes are all about.

> 1 We **believe** that he **will** be better soon.
>
> 2 I **think** he **is** the best player of our team.
>   I **thought** he **was** the best player of our team.
>
> 3 Everyone **knows** that *the Korean War **broke out** in 1950*.

Meaning & Use

1_ 주절과 종속절로 구성되는 복문에서는 시제 일치의 문제가 일어난다. 이때 주절의 시제가 현재이면 종속절에는 어떤 시제든 올 수 있다.

I know he is a soldier.

I know he was a soldier.

I know he will be a soldier some day.

2_ 주절의 시제가 과거이면 종속절에는 과거 또는 과거 완료가 오는 것이 원칙이다.

He thinks he lost his concert ticket.

→ He thought he had lost his concert ticket.

I believe he will come to the party.

→ I believed he would come to the party.

3_ 불변의 진리나 과학적 사실은 언제나 현재시제로 표현한다. 반면 역사적 사실은 과거시제를 쓰는 것이 원칙이다.

He proved that *the earth is round*.

cf. Ancient people believed that *the earth was flat*.

Our history teacher said that Columbus discovered America in 1492.

Key point_ 종속절의 조동사

학교 내신시험에서는 주절이 과거인 경우에 종속절의 조동사도 과거형이 되어야 한다는 점을 종종 출제한다. 다음 Unit에서 다룰 화법전환과 관련해서도 중요한 사항이므로, 정확히 익혀 두어야 한다.

Hannah thought that Robert would come. (O)

Hannah thought that Robert will come. (X)

Exercises

A 적절한 것을 괄호 안에서 고르시오.

1 She (is, was) watching video when I entered the room.

2 Tom said that he (drinks, had drunk) the rest of the milk last night.

3 My brother promised that he (will, would) bring me a present.

4 I was sure that she (will, would) be a musician.

5 Catherine insisted that it (take, took) one hour for her to come here.

6 It is certain that Brandon (breaks, broke) the window the other day.

7 I didn't know that Kate (is, was) very sick.

B 밑줄 친 부분이 어법에 맞으면 T, 맞지 않으면 F라고 쓰고 맞게 고치시오.

1 He said that he <u>had gone</u> to the movies
with her.　　　　　　　　　　　　　　　( )　_____

2 I heard that Joan <u>will go</u> to Africa.　　　( )　_____

3 He said there <u>will be</u> a thunderstorm.　　( )　_____

4 He promised me that he <u>would visit</u> the
nursing home.　　　　　　　　　　　　　( )　_____

5 I didn't know that he <u>lies</u> to me.　　　　　( )　_____

6 Didn't you know that I <u>am</u> born in January?　( )　_____

7 They recognized that they <u>made</u> a big
mistake.　　　　　　　　　　　　　　　　( )　_____

C 다음 글의 밑줄 친 부분 중, 어법상 틀린 것은?

The man believed that holding a flower festival ①<u>was</u> a bad idea. First of
all, he thought that such an event ②<u>will</u> make the school dirty. After a
festival, people would not ③<u>care</u> about flowers. So they would put them
anywhere in the school. Second, he didn't like the idea of ④<u>having</u> fun.
The man didn't want to see people ⑤<u>have</u> fun. He believed that it was a
foolish thing to do.

Form

1 Paul said to her, **"I love you."**
Paul told her that **he loved her**.

2 June said to Alex, **"I will quit school."**
→ June told Alex that **she would** quit school.

3 He said, **"I moved here last year."**
→ He said **he had moved there the previous year**.

Meaning & Use

1_ 어떤 사람이 한 말을 다른 사람에게 전달하는 것을 화법이라고 하는데, 말한 사람의 말을 그대로 인용부호("") 안에 넣어 전달하는 직접화법과 전달하는 사람의 입장에서 나타내는 간접화법으로 나뉜다.

He said, "I want to see a movie." (직접화법)

He said that he wanted to see a movie. (간접화법)

2_ 직접화법은 다음과 같은 방법으로 간접화법으로 전환할 수 있다. (평서문)

- 필요할 때는 전달동사를 바꾸고 (say to → tell),
- 인칭대명사를 상황에 맞게 바꾼 다음,
- 시제 일치를 적용하고,
- 시간을 나타내는 부사를 적절히 바꾼다.

Jimmy said[1], "We[2] majored[3] in English literature."

→ Jimmy said[1] that they[2] had majored[3] in English literature.

3_ 화법 전환에서 주의해야 할 부사 표현은 다음과 같다.

- here → there
- this → that
- now → then, at the time
- ago → before
- today → that day
- tomorrow → the next day [the following day]
- last year → the previous year[the year before]

Mark said to[1] me, "I[2] will[3] go to Paris tomorrow[4]."

→ Mark told[1] me that he[2] would[3] go to Paris the next day[4].

Exercises

A 적절한 것을 괄호 안에서 고르시오.

1 Dad said that he would be back (tomorrow, the following day).

2 He (said, told) to us, "I'll be going with you if you want."

3 She (said, told) to me, "Let's go hiking tomorrow."

4 The reporter said, "It (is, was) going to rain tonight."

5 Mom announced, "We're going to the park (tomorrow, the next day)."

6 Susan said the soup (is, was) too salty.

B 화법 전환이 올바르면 T, 올바르지 않으면 F라고 쓰고 올바르게 고치시오.

1 She said, "I was sick yesterday." → She said that I was sick yesterday.

( ) _____

2 "I'm hungry," says Sammy. → Sammy says that I'm hungry.

( ) _____

3 Bod said to us, "You have to finish this in an hour."

→ Bob said to us that we have to finish that in an hour.

( ) _____

4 The boy said, "I want to have a cat."

→ The boy said that he wanted to have a cat.

( ) _____

5 He said, "We're getting married here."

→ He said that we're getting married there.

( ) _____

C 다음 글의 밑줄 친 부분 중, 어법상 틀린 것은?

Do you know ① how old Satchel Paige was when he played baseball for the last time? He was 59. Can you ② believe that? But it is true. As a pitcher, he played for the Kansas City Athletics. The team played against the Boston Red Sox. Satchel pitched three innings of shut-out ball. How ③ could he be so strong at the age of 59? He said, "④ Age doesn't matter." Do you agree wlth hlm? Anyway, Satchel told us that elderly people ⑤ want to do many things.

Form

> 1 Ellen **said to** me, "**What** do you want to eat for lunch?"
>   → Ellen **asked** me **what I wanted** to eat for lunch.
>
> 2 He **said**, "**Do** you speak French?"
>   → He **asked if[whether] I spoke** French.

Meaning & Use

1 _ 의문문의 화법 전환은 본래 의문문이 의문사가 있는 의문문인가 의문사가 없는 의문문인가에 따라 달라진다. 의문사가 있는 의문문의 화법 전환은 다음과 같다.

- 전달동사 say (to)를 ask로 바꾸고,
- 의문문의 어순을 [의문사+주어+동사]로 바꾸되, 의문사가 주어이면 [의문사+동사]로 한 다음,
- 인칭대명사와 시제를 상황에 맞게 바꾼다.

He said to[1] me, "What is[2] your[3] favorite song?"

→ He asked[1] me what my[3] favorite song was[2].

He said[1], "Why are[2] you[3] late again?"

→ He asked[1] why I[3] was[2] late again.

The man said to me, "What[2] bothers[3] you?" (의문사 주어)

→ The man asked me what[2]bothered[3] me.

2 _ 의문사가 없는 의문문의 화법 전환은 다음과 같다.

- 전달동사 say (to)를 ask로 바꾸고,
- 의문문의 어순을 [if / whether+주어+동사]로 바꾼 다음,
- 인칭대명사와 시제를 상황에 맞게 바꾼다.

The girl said to me, "Are you fond of skiing?"

→ The girl asked me if [whether] I was fond of skiing.

Davis said to me, "Have you ever been to Italy?"

→ Davis asked me if [whether] I had ever been to Italy.

Exercises

A   적절한 것을 괄호 안에서 고르시오.

1   She (said to, asked) me if I went to the party.

2   I asked my mom (who, if) the guests were still there.

3   I wonder (if, as) you can help us with this tomorrow.

4   Dad asked me what I (want, wanted) to get for my birthday.

5   Jimmy asked her if (she kept, did she keep) a diary.

B   화법 전환이 올바르면 T, 올바르지 않으면 F라고 쓰고 올바르게 고치시오.

1   The doctor said to me, "Do you have a fever?"

     → The doctor asked me whether I had a fever.

     ( ) _____

2   She said to me, "Where do you live?"

     → She asked me where do you live.

     ( ) _____

3   He said to me, "Do you like reading comic books?"

     → He asked me if I like reading comic books.

     ( ) _____

4   My friend asked me, "Why are you so angry?"

     → My friend asked me why you were so angry.

     ( ) _____

5   She asked him, "Do you speak Spanish?"

     → She asked him whether you spoke Spanish.

     ( ) _____

C   다음 글의 밑줄 친 부분 중, 어법상 틀린 것은?

If someone asks me ① what is my wish, I'll answer, without hesitation, "Peace in the whole world." You may think my answer ② is too abstract. But peace is not merely an abstract concept. It is what we can feel deep in our hearts and ③ experience in everyday life. For instance, when we ④ get along with each other, we can ⑤ sense the friendly and peaceful atmosphere among us.

Form

> 1 I said to him, "Turn off the lights."
>   → I **told** him to **turn off** the lights.
>
> 2 The doctor said to her, "Try to lose some weight."
>   → The doctor **advised** her **to try to lose** some weight.
>
> 3 She said to him, "Please lend me your umbrella."
>   → She **asked** him **to lend** her his umbrella.

Meaning & Use

1_ 전달하는 문장이 명령문인 경우, 전달 동사를 명령문의 내용에 맞게 바꾸고, 피전달문의 동사를 to부정사로 바꾼다. 또한 인칭대명사와 동사의 시제, 부사구 등을 적절히 바꾼다. 전달하는 내용이 지시나 명령일 경우 전달동사를 tell, order 등으로 한다. 부정명령문일 경우에는 to부정사 앞에 not을 붙인다.

He said to us, "Be quiet." → He told us to be quiet.

She said to her secretary, "Bring me the paper on the desk."

→ She ordered her secretary to bring her the paper on the desk.

My brother said to me, "Don't bother me."

→ My brother told me not to bother him.

2_ 전달하는 내용이 충고나 조언일 경우 전달동사를 advise, warn 등으로 한다.

The doctor said to me, "Exercise regularly."

→ The doctor advised me to exercise regularly.

3_ 전달하는 내용이 부탁이나 요청인 경우에는 전달동사를 ask, beg, request 등으로 한다.
Let's로 시작하는 제안문일 경우에는 전달동사를 suggest, propose 등으로 하고 동사는
V-ing 형이나 [that+we+동사원형]으로 한다.

She said to me, "Please lend me a pen."

→ She asked[begged] me to lend her a pen.

He said to me, "Let's go to the ball park."

→ He suggested going to the ball park.

→ He suggested[proposed] (to me) that we go to the ball park.

Exercises

A   다음은 직접화법을 간접화법으로 전환한 것이다. 적절한 것을 괄호 안에서 고르시오.

1   Mom said to me, "Clean your room first."

→ Mom (told, suggested) me to clean my room first.

2   The doctor said to his patient, "Take this pill after each meal."

→ The doctor told his patient (take, to take) that pill after each meal.

3   She said to me, "Please wake me up tomorrow morning."

→ She asked me to wake (me, her) up the next morning.

4   My friend said, "Let's go swimming."

→ My friend suggested (to go, going) swimming.

B   화법 전환이 올바르면 T, 올바르지 않으면 F라고 쓰고 올바르게 고치시오.

1   He said to me, "Bring me some food."

→ He asked me bring me some food.

( ) _____

2   I said to her, "Let's play chess." → I proposed to her that we play chess.

( ) _____

3   I said to him, "Go home before dark."

→ I advised him going home before dark.

( ) _____

4   Dad said to me, "Don't bother me." → Dad didn't warn me to bother him.

( ) _____

C   다음 글의 밑줄 친 부분 중, 어법상 틀린 것은?

Once upon a time, there lived a little girl. She loved ① to play and dance, but she had to work all day long, because her family was so poor. One day, when she was working, a fairy appeared and invited her ② to dance together. She danced with the fairy, but was ③ worried about her work. At sunset, the fairy disappeared. The next day, the fairy appeared again and ④ promised to work for her. And the fairy gave the girl a small box. The fairy told the girl ⑤ to not look into it until she got home.

Chapter Review

A 잘못된 곳을 고치시오.

1 Rick and I am of an age.

2 Either Mr. Simpson or Ms. White have to stay in the office.

3 Every boy and girl have his or her goal.

4 Not only you but also he are invited to the party.

5 Both Jim and I was late for school today.

6 A quarter of them is movie magazines.

7 He knows that *Romeo and Juliet* were written by Shakespeare.

8 The rest of the water were split on the floor.

9 He promised that he will come.

10 She said that she have seen the movie yesterday.

11 The CDs I lent you is not mine.

12 She said she went swimming every morning these days.

13 The boss told to him, "You're fired."

14 Mom said that she wants to see me.

15 He told that he will play tennis with me the next day.

16 We visited our grandparents who will live in the country.

17 Some of the passengers was injured in the car accident.

18 One of the club members are missing.

19 She asked him if he knows her sister.

20 A stranger asked me if could you tell me where's the nearest bank.

21 He asked me how was my day.

22 She asked me if her hair looks nice.

23 My mother says me when I would come home.

24 My daughter asked me to buy me a new dress.

25 I asked her help me with the problem.

B (A), (B), (C)의 각 괄호 안에서 어법에 맞는 표현을 골라 짝지은 것으로 가장 적절한 것은?

Penguins are very strange. Of course, they are birds, but they cannot fly. This is because their bones are too heavy. Those heavy bones are good for (A) [to swim, swimming], though. This is very important because they spend most of their time at sea. Most penguins live at the South Pole, which (B) [is, are] a very cold place. Don't penguins feel cold? Usually, they don't. Their feathers keep them warm. But sometimes it is so cold that penguins (C) [need, needs] to gather to keep one another warm. In that sense, they know how to live together.

	(A)	(B)	(C)
①	to swim	are	needs
②	swimming	are	need
③	to swim	is	needs
④	swimming	is	need
⑤	swimming	is	needs

C 다음 글의 밑줄 친 부분 중, 어법상 틀린 것은?

Once upon a time, there ① lived a beautiful fairy. One day, she came across a man and ② fell in love with him at once. When the master of fairies found out that the fairy loved the man, he got angry and told them ③ to see not each other again. The fairy was very sad and cried every day. ④ Touched by her love, the master finally allowed them ⑤ to meet once a year. The day fell on the Harvest Moon Festival.

D 다음 밑줄 친 부분에 가장 적절한 것을 고르시오.

1 Either Steve or his wife _____ once a professor.

a. is   b. are

c. was   d. were

2 Bread and butter _____ my favorite.

a. is   b. are

c. will   d. does

3 Not only my brother but also I _____ a writer.

a. am   b. is

c. are   d. were

4 The papers in the box _____ for recycling.

a. is   b. are

c. was   d. be

5 Each of the members _____ doing their own job last night.

a. is   b. are

c. was   d. were

6 He promised he _____ that place the next day.

a. leaves   b. left

c. will leave   d. would leave

7 _____ of the participants is unknown.

a. Many   b. Some

c. A number   d. The number

8 Sixty miles _____ a long distance for a child.

a. is   b. are

c. have been   d. were

9 He said that he _____ me a ride.

a. gives   b. will give

c. would give   d. have given

10 We learned the earth _____ around the sun.

a. move   b. moves

c. moved   d. would move

11 They said they _____ to church every Sunday when they were young.

a. go   b. went

c. will go   d. are going

12 Dad said that he _____ Chicago the next day.

a. visits   b. visit

c. will visit   d. would visit

13 My boyfriend _____ me when I would go to Canada.

a. said   b. told

c. asked   d. advised

14 Her boss asked her _____ she could finish the project in time.

a. when   b. whether

c. what   d. as soon as

15 I _____ if she had ever been to Rome.

a. said to   b. wondered

c. knew   d. told

16 He asked her how long she _____ in this country.

a. would stay   b. stays

c. will stay   d. stay

17 I wondered _____ I could finish the large pizza all by myself.

a. as   b. if

c. what   d. how many

18 The king _____ his servant to find him gold.

a. ordered   b. said

c. proposed   d. suggested

19 My friend asked me _____ shopping with her.

a. go   b. going

c. to go   d. should go

20 His boss commanded him _____ after work.

a. stay   b. staying

c. to stay   d. should stay

불규칙 동사표

원형	과거형	과거분사	원형	과거형	과거분사
arise	arose	arisen	fall	fell	fallen
bear	bore	borne	feed	fed	fed
beat	beat	beaten	feel	felt	felt
become	became	become	fight	fought	fought
begin	began	begun	find	found	found
bend	bent	bent	flee	fled	fled
bet	bet	bet	fly	flew	flown
bind	bound	bound	forget	forgot	forgotten
bite	bit	bitten	forgive	forgave	forgiven
blow	blew	blown	freeze	froze	frozen
break	broke	broken	get	got	gotten
bring	brought	brought	give	gave	given
broadcast	broadcast	broadcast	go	went	gone
build	built	built	grow	grew	grown
*burn	burnt	burnt	hang	hung	hung
burst	burst	burst	**hang	hanged	hanged
buy	bought	bought	have	had	had
cast	cast	cast	hear	heard	heard
catch	caught	caught	hide	hid	hidden
choose	chose	chosen	hit	hit	hit
come	came	come	hold	held	held
cost	cost	cost	hurt	hurt	hurt
cut	cut	cut	keep	kept	kept
deal	dealt	dealt	kneel	knelt	knelt
dig	dug	dug	know	knew	known
do	did	done	lay	laid	laid
draw	drew	drawn	lead	led	led
drink	drank	drunk	*lean	leant	leant
drive	drove	driven	*leap	leapt	leapt
eat	ate	eaten	*learn	learnt	learnt

* burn, lean, leap, learn : 규칙변화도 가능
** hang: "교수형에 처하다"라는 뜻일 때는 위와 같이 규칙변화

원형	과거형	과거분사	원형	과거형	과거분사
leave	left	left	show	showed	shown
lend	lent	lent	shrink	shrank	shrunk
let	let	let	shut	shut	shut
lie	lay	lain	sing	sang	sung
***lie	lied	lied	sink	sank	sunk
lose	lost	lost	sit	sat	sat
make	made	made	sleep	slept	slept
meet	met	met	sow	sowed	sown
mistake	mistook	mistaken	speak	spoke	spoken
mow	mowed	mown	spend	spent	spent
oversleep	overslept	overslept	******spill	spilt	spilt
pay	paid	paid	spread	spread	spread
prove	proved	proven	spring	sprang	sprung
put	put	put	stand	stood	stood
quit	quit	quit	steal	stole	stolen
****read	read	read	strike	struck	struck
ride	rode	ridden	sweep	swept	swept
rise	rose	risen	swim	swam	swum
run	ran	run	take	took	taken
say	said	said	teach	taught	taught
see	saw	seen	tear	tore	torn
seek	sought	sought	tell	told	told
sell	sold	sold	think	thought	thought
send	sent	sent	throw	threw	thrown
set	set	set	wake	woke	woken
shake	shook	shaken	wear	wore	worn
shed	shed	shed	weep	wept	wept
shine	shone	shone	win	won	won
*****shine	shined	shined	wind	wound	wound
shoot	shot	shot	write	wrote	written

***lie: "거짓말하다"라는 뜻일 때는 위와 같이 규칙변화
****read: 과거형과 과거분사의 발음이 red와 똑같음
*****shine: "광택을 내다"라는 뜻일 때는 위와 같이 규칙 변화
******spill: 규칙변화도 가능

TOP GRAMMAR 중급-1

중쇄 펴낸날 ㅣ 2010년 12월 22일

지은이 ㅣ 김 옥 정

펴낸이 ㅣ 강 남 현

펴낸곳 ㅣ 월드컴출판사

등록 ㅣ 2000년 1월 17일

주소 ㅣ 서울시 구로구 구로동 222-8 (우편번호 152-848)

코오롱 디지탈타워 빌란트Ⅱ 1005호

전화 ㅣ 02)3273-4300(대표)

팩스 ㅣ 02)3273-4303

홈페이지 ㅣ www.wcbooks.co.kr

이메일 ㅣ wc4300@yahoo.co.kr

TOP GRAMMAR

중급 - 1

For Intermediate Students

Workbook

WorldCom

Chapter 1

동사의 종류

A 다음 중 알맞은 단어를 빈칸에 써 넣으시오. (전치사가 필요한 경우 써 넣으시오.)

| marry   agree   join   apologized   resembles |

1 He _____ me for being late again.

2 Why don't you _____ our club?

3 I don't _____ with you on the matter.

4 My younger sister _____ my grandmother.

5 Mr. Johnson will _____ my cousin, Jessica.

B 다음 중 어법상 옳은 문장을 있는 대로 고르시오.

① How long have you waited me here?

② Please do not enter this room.

③ He and his staff will arrive Seoul in a minute.

④ They don't want to discuss the problem any more.

⑤ Could you explain of the rule to me?

C 다음 주어진 단어를 이용하여 영작하시오.

1 카페인은 여러 가지 면에서 인체에 영향을 준다. (affect, in many ways, your body)

→ Caffeine _____ .

2 그녀는 항상 무언가에 대해 불평한다. (complains, something, about)

→ She always _____ .

3 그 방에 있는 사람들은 모두 나의 의견에 반대했다. (my suggestion, opposed, in the room)

→ Everybody _____ .

4 나는 내 여동생을 돌봐야 한다. (take care, my younger sister, of)

→ I should _____ .

5 그는 회의에 참석하기 위해 나갔다. (went out, the meeting, to attend)

→ He _____ .

2. 완전동사 vs. 불완전동사

A 다음 중 알맞은 단어를 써 넣으시오. 또한 빈칸에 들어갈 단어가 목적어이면 〈목〉, 보어이면 〈보〉라고 쓰시오.

better	pilot	lonely	e-mails	political problems

1 The man looks so _____ .   [   ]

2 My son became a _____ .   [   ]

3 He wrote _____to his students.   [   ]

4 They discussed _____all night.   [   ]

5 Now I feel _____for it.   [   ]

B 다음 중 어법상 옳은 문장을 있는 대로 고르시오.

① We made a cake for her birthday.

② This soup tastes bad.

③ All of a sudden, the woman cried bitter.

④ I remained silent because I didn't know what to say.

⑤ He seems to be very strangely today.

C 다음 주어진 단어를 이용하여 영작하시오.

1 그녀는 나이에 비해 무척 젊어 보였다. (her, very, looked, age, young, for)

→ She _____ .

2 아무도 내 질문에 대답하지 않았다 (my, answered, question)

→ Nobody _____ .

3 그의 말에 그녀는 얼굴을 붉혔다. (turned, at, remark, red, his)

→ Her face _____ .

4 오늘은 누나가 우리에게 저녁 식사를 만들어 주었다. (dinner, us, for, cooked)

→ Today my sister _____ .

5 나는 어제 큰 여행용 가방을 샀다. (big, yesterday, suitcase, bought, a)

→ I _____ .

A 다음 빈칸에 알맞은 전치사를 써 넣으시오. 필요 없을 경우 빈칸으로 두시오.

1 Rebecca sent _____ me a love letter.

2 We bought an electric shaver _____ my father.

3 Can I ask a favor _____ you?

4 Mrs. Lee taught math _____ us.

5 I'd like to show something _____ you.

B 다음 중 어법상 옳은 문장을 있는 대로 고르시오.

① The boy asked a question to his teacher.
② Will you get me something hot to drink?
③ I played songs for the children.
④ He sold his old bike for his friend.
⑤ I'll buy you a drink tonight.

C 다음 주어진 단어를 이용하여 영작하시오.

1 할머니께서 내게 그녀의 결혼반지를 주셨다. (to, ring, me, her, gave, wedding)

→ My grandmother _____.

2 그는 여자 친구를 위해 책을 샀다. (a, bought, for, his, book, girlfriend)

→ He _____.

3 당신 전화번호를 제게 알려주시겠어요? (give, your, me, phone number)

→ Can you _____ ?

4 우리 형은 나에게 영어를 가르쳐준다. (teaches, English, me)

→ My brother _____.

5 이 소포를 제인에게 보내려고 한다. (this, send, to, package)

→ I'm going to _____ Jane.

A 다음 주어진 동사를 문맥에 맞게 고치시오.

1 My parents expected me _____ (become) a lawyer.

2 They saw him _____ (hold) a large bag.

3 Mom won't allow you _____ (go) to the party.

4 He made her _____ (understand) a lot of things.

5 She had the kids _____ (get) out of the attic.

B 다음 중 어법상 옳은 문장을 있는 대로 고르시오.

① He made me carry his baggage.

② Many children called him Uncle Tom.

③ I saw a man climbed over the wall.

④ You'll find this book interested.

⑤ We heard her name called.

C 다음 주어진 단어를 이용하여 영작하시오.

1 우리는 울타리를 흰색으로 칠하도록 했다. (fence, white, had, the, painted)

→ We _____.

2 나는 아기가 우는 소리를 듣지 못했다. (not, the, did, baby, cry, hear)

→ I _____.

3 그녀는 고양이를 돌봐달라고 부탁했다. (her, of, asked, take, me, cat, care, to)

→ She _____.

4 나는 당신이 이 직책을 맡아줬으면 합니다. (to, position, you, take, this)

→ I'd like _____.

5 나는 사람들을 웃게 하는 방법을 발견했다. (way, make, laugh, people, a, to)

→ I've found _____.

Chapter 2

시제

A   다음 주어진 동사를 문맥에 맞게 고치시오.

1   Water _____ (freeze) at 0°C.

2   My sister _____ (be) sick in bed now.

3   Carl _____ (go) swimming every Saturday morning.

4   If you _____ (want) to come with me, just call me.

5   I _____ (have) a job interview tomorrow

B   다음 중 어법상 옳은 문장을 있는 대로 고르시오.

① Call me as soon as you'll arrive in Seoul.

② If it's out of stock, we will let you know.

③ The next World Cup is held in South Africa.

④ He goes on a business trip next week.

⑤ The capital of the United States will be Washington D.C.

C   다음 주어진 단어를 이용하여 영작하시오.

1   막차는 오후 11시 40분에 출발합니다. (at, bus, leaves, the, 11:40 p.m., last)

→ _____ .

2   우주비행사가 되고 싶다면 이 책을 읽어보시오. (astronaut, want, be, an, to)

→ If you _____ , read this book.

3   그녀는 매일 아침 우유 한 잔을 마신다. (morning, drinks, a glass of milk, every)

→ She _____ .

4   물은 수소와 산소로 구성되어 있다. (of, oxygen, consists, hydrogen, and)

→ Water _____ .

5   그는 겨울마다 스키장에 간다. (a ski resort, every, goes, winter, to)

→ He _____ .

2. 과거시제

A 다음 주어진 동사를 문맥에 맞게 고치시오.

1 I _____ (major) in English literature when I was in college.

2 It _____ (snow) heavily last night.

3 My friend and I _____ (travel) to Europe last month.

4 Thomas Edison _____ (invent) the light bulb in 1879.

5 They _____ (get) married twenty years ago.

B 다음 중 어법상 옳은 문장을 있는 대로 고르시오.

① They came here last night.
② My parents are Korean but I was born in Chicago.
③ One of my friends has moved Australia several years ago.
④ I'm so tired because I slept only four hours last night.
⑤ When I am young, I used to play with toys.

C 다음 주어진 단어를 이용하여 영작하시오.

1 나는 어제 노트북 컴퓨터를 샀다. (a, yesterday, notebook computer, bought)

→ I _____.

2 그 작가는 작년에 소설 한 권을 썼다. (year, a, wrote, last, novel)

→ The writer _____.

3 그녀는 다이어트를 하기로 결심했다. (to, on a diet, decided, go)

→ She _____.

4 기자는 그녀에게 새 작품에 관해 물어보았다. (her, her, about, work, asked, new)

→ The reporter _____.

5 그들은 10년 전에 이곳으로 이사했다. (ten, here, ago, moved, years)

→ They _____.

A 다음 주어진 동사를 문맥에 맞게 고치시오. (단, will이나 be going to를 사용한 미래시제로 만드시오.)

1 If you take this pill, you _____ (feel) better.

2 It's so cloudy. It _____ (rain) soon.

3 If you keep it a secret, I _____ (tell) you about it.

4 Let's go out for dinner. I _____ (treat) you tonight.

5 We know her birthday is coming up, and we _____ (have) a party for her.

B 다음 중 어법상 옳은 문장을 있는 대로 고르시오.

① I'm going to turn thirteen next month.

② If it snows tomorrow, we'll go to the ski resort.

③ We're going to watch the movie this Friday.

④ If you will need more help, just tell me.

⑤ When will you arrive here?

C 다음 주어진 단어를 이용하여 영작하시오.

1 그녀는 보스턴에서 1년 더 머물 것이다. (year, stay, in, one, will, Boston, more)

→ She _____.

2 나는 그 일을 혼자서 하지 않을 것이다. (by, not, do, work, will, myself, the)

→ I _____.

3 내일 날씨는 덥고 습할 것이다. (tomorrow, be, it, humid, will, and, hot)

→ _____.

4 답을 찾으면 알려주세요. (find, if, answer, you, the)

→ _____, let me know.

5 그는 캐나다로 갈 것이다. (go, he, Canada, will, to)

→ _____.

4. 현재완료

A 다음 주어진 동사를 문맥에 맞게 고치시오.

1 He _____ (finish) the work just now.

2 How long _____ (you, stay) here so far?

3 Greg _____ (be) my tutor since I was in the 4th grade.

4 I _____ (not, read) the article for the assignment yet.

5 My girlfriend _____ (go) to Italy last year.

B 다음 중 어법상 옳은 문장을 있는 대로 고르시오.

① He has lost his bag a couple of days ago.
② My family have lived here since last summer.
③ They've not finished painting the walls yet.
④ I've worked for the company since I graduate from college.
⑤ Have you gone to Paris before?

C 다음 주어진 단어를 이용하여 영작하시오.

1 나는 뉴욕에 두 번 갔다 온 적이 있다. (to, have, New York, been)

→ I _____ twice.

2 그는 아무것도 먹지 못했다. (not, all, eaten, has, at)

→ He _____.

3 우리는 3주간 그 프로젝트를 해왔다. (on, project, weeks, for, worked, the, three)

→ We've _____.

4 그를 만나지 못한 지 10년이 되었다. (met, ten, him, for, not, years, have)

→ I _____.

5 나는 그 책을 다 읽었다. (reading, have, book, finished, the)

→ I _____.

A 다음 주어진 동사를 문맥에 맞게 고치시오. (단, 미래완료와 과거완료 중에 하나를 사용하시오.)

1 We _____ (live) in Sydney for ten years before we moved here.

2 He _____ (finish) the work before the deadline.

3 She said she _____ (never, meet) him before.

4 The game _____ (end) by the time you arrive.

5 Michael _____ (learn) Japanese for a year before his trip.

B 다음 중 어법상 옳은 문장을 있는 대로 고르시오.

① I've not eaten anything before you came here.

② He'll have cleaned the room by the time you arrive.

③ We will have reached our destination by tomorrow night.

④ I'll have called you several times since yesterday.

⑤ Eric had taught in a middle school before he started his own business.

C 다음 주어진 단어를 이용하여 영작하시오.

1 내가 전화를 했을 때 그는 이미 사무실을 떠났다. (office, already, left, the, had)

→ He _____ when I called him.

2 그녀는 내가 그곳에 이르기 전에 책을 읽었었다. (had, book, read, she, a)

→ _____ before I got there.

3 나는 디지털 카메라를 사용했었다. (used, a, I, digital camera, had)

→ _____ .

4 그는 내년이면 이 회사에서 근무한 지 30년이 될 것이다.
(worked, thirty, will, company, have, for, for, this, years)

→ He _____ by next year.

5 우리 부모님은 한 번도 외국에 나가보신 적이 없었다. (been, had, abroad, never)

→ My parents _____ .

6. 현재진행형·과거진행형

A 다음 주어진 동사를 문맥에 맞게 고치시오.

1 The waiter _____ (mop) the floor right now.

2 Mom _____ (cook) in the kitchen right now.

3 I _____ (do) my assignment when he called me.

4 The pink cap _____ (belong) to me.

5 Sorry, but I _____ (not, understand) what you mean by that.

B 다음 중 어법상 옳은 문장을 있는 대로 고르시오.

① A man is looking up the sky.

② A little boy is chasing the dog.

③ We were playing computer games when he visited us.

④ The athletes are seeming very tired.

⑤ I'm not knowing what you mean.

C 다음 주어진 단어를 이용하여 영작하시오.

1 나는 공포 영화를 보고 있었다. (horror, watching, movie, a was)

→ I _____.

2 그들은 점심을 먹고 있었다. (lunch, they, having, were)

→ _____.

3 그는 트럭을 몰고 있었다. (driving, he, truck, was, a)

→ _____.

4 새 선생님은 좋은 것 같다. (the, seems, teacher, nice, new)

→ _____.

5 나는 집에서 잠을 자고 있었다. (was, home, sleeping, at, I)

→ _____.

Chapter 3

태

A 다음 주어진 동사를 문맥에 맞게 고치시오.

1 This sculpture was _____ (make) by Leonardo da Vinci.

2 Tarry was _____ (hit) by a ball during the golf competition.

3 My father was _____ (transfer) to the L.A. branch office.

4 The song was _____ (sing) by Sarah Brightman.

5 George W. Bush was _____ (reelect) President of the United States.

B 다음 중 어법상 옳은 문장을 있는 대로 고르시오.

① This play was first performed in 1972.

② Somebody was stolen my notebook in the library.

③ They were nominated for the awards.

④ The cottonseed first introduced by Moon Ik-Jeom in the 14th century.

⑤ She was paid $4,000 a month when she worked as a copywriter.

C 다음 주어진 단어를 이용하여 영작하시오.

1 우리는 그 소식을 듣고 기뻤다. (the, pleased, to, news, hear, were)

→ We _____.

2 이 초상화는 남편이 그린 것이다. (husband, by, painted, my, was)

→ This portrait _____.

3 그 방은 초록색과 흰색으로 장식되었다. (and, in, green, decorated, white, was)

→ The room _____.

4 이 식탁은 일본인 장인이 만든 것이다. (by, Japanese, made, craftsman, a, was)

→ This table _____.

5 우리 웹사이트가 지난 주에 십대 해커들의 공격을 받았다.
(attacked, hackers, was, teenage, week, by, last)

→ Our web site _____.

2. 4형식 문형의 수동태

A 다음 빈칸에 들어갈 알맞은 전치사를 쓰시오.

1 This letter was not sent _____ her.

2 A new computer was delivered _____ me.

3 German was taught _____ us by James.

4 The bike was bought _____ my younger brother.

5 A lot of gifts were given _____ her on her birthday.

B 다음 중 어법상 옳은 문장을 있는 대로 고르시오.

① The girl was given a new dress.

② The speaker was asked some private questions.

③ African culture was taught of the college students by Harold.

④ Some books were bought to the poor children.

⑤ The cookies were given of the sisters.

C 다음 주어진 단어를 이용하여 영작하시오.

1 그 박스는 우리 삼촌에게 온 것이었다. (uncle, sent, to, was, my)

→ The box _____ .

2 그의 그림은 딸에게 주어졌다. (daughter, to, was, his, given)

→ His picture _____ .

3 그 선물은 제인을 위해 산 것이었다. (for, was, bought, Jane)

→ The gift _____ .

4 우리는 수학을 메리 선생님으로부터 배웠다. (taught, by, were, math, Mary)

→ We _____ .

5 그는 어려운 질문을 받았다. (asked, question, hard, was, a)

→ He _____ .

A 다음 문장을 수동태로 바꿀 때 빈칸에 알맞은 말을 써 넣으시오.

1 His mom made Jacob a doctor.

→ _____ was made a doctor by his mom.

2 The coach asked me to join the team.

→ I was asked _____ the team by the coach.

3 I saw my classmate peeping through the locked door.

→ My classmate was seen _____ through the locked door.

B 다음 중 어법상 옳은 문장을 있는 대로 고르시오.

① He was expected promoted to director.
② Please let her to go.
③ I heard the choir singing in the church.
④ We considered him to be a great politician.
⑤ You are not allowed to bring those items inside.

C 다음 주어진 단어를 이용하여 영작하시오.

1 내가 우리 반 반장으로 선출되었다. (president, class, elected, my, was, of)

→ I _____ .

2 우리는 학교에서 교복을 입어야 했다. (to, school, uniforms, were, wear, made)

→ We _____ at school.

3 어젯밤 그가 그 가게로 침입한 것이 보였다. (seen, store, break, was, the, to, into)

→ He _____ last night.

4 그녀는 뛰어난 작가로 간주되었다. (excellent, considered, writer, was, an)

→ She _____ .

5 그 신약은 폐암을 치료할 것으로 여겨졌다. (to, lung cancer, was, cure, believed)

→ The new medicine _____ .

4. 완료 및 진행형 수동태

A 다음 주어진 동사를 이용하여 괄호 안의 지시대로 변형시키시오.

1 The music _____ (play) by Jefferson. (현재진행형)

2 The building _____ (construct) by next month. (미래완료)

3 The problem _____ (solve) by my cousin Billy. (현재완료)

4 He said the movie *E.T.* _____ (direct) by Steven Spielberg. (과거완료)

5 The room _____ (use) as a store at that time. (과거진행형)

B 다음 중 어법상 옳은 문장을 있는 대로 고르시오.

① The cookies are being cooked in the oven.

② They had been punished for being late.

③ The pictures were being take by a professional photographer.

④ The thief has been catch by a pedestrian.

⑤ All the workers knew they tested being.

C 다음 주어진 단어를 이용하여 영작하시오.

1 그 다리는 건설 중이었다. (built, being, was)

→ The bridge _____.

2 그 말은 기둥에 매여지고 있었다. (to, being, post, tied, the, was)

→ The horse _____.

3 세 명의 소년들이 그 구멍을 파고 있다. (three, being, by, is, boys, dug)

→ The hole _____.

4 스파게티는 데워졌다. (been, has, heated)

→ The spaghetti _____.

5 그 영화는 평론가들로부터 평을 받았다. (by, been, critics, reviewed, has, the)

→ The movie _____.

A 다음 주어진 동사를 문맥에 맞게 고치시오.

1 His room is _____ (fill) with computer magazines.

2 I think the magician is _____ (disappoint) with his own performance.

3 I'm not _____ (interest) any kinds of parties.

4 Everybody was _____ (amaze) at the sudden change.

5 He was _____ (frighten) of what he heard.

B 다음 중 어법상 옳은 문장을 있는 대로 고르시오.

① The writer was worried by his new novel.
② I'm so bored with Mr. Kim's class.
③ I hope you're pleased with our service.
④ Karen is experienced in the advertising industry.
⑤ My mother has been married with my father for ten years.

C 다음 주어진 단어를 이용하여 영작하시오.

1 당신은 일에 만족하십니까? (with, job, satisfied, your)

→ Are you _____?

2 지붕이 흰색 타일로 덮여 있다. (tiles, covered, white, is, with)

→ The roof _____.

3 명사란 많은 사람들에게 잘 알려진 사람을 일컫는다. (many, to, people, is, well-known)

→ A celebrity is someone who _____.

4 그는 발표에 대해 걱정했다. (his, worried, presentation, about, was)

→ He _____.

5 그의 연구에 관심이 있는 사람은 거의 없다. (his, are, in, research, interested)

→ Few _____.

Chapter 4

조동사

A   다음 중 알맞은 단어를 빈칸에 써 넣으시오.

bike	drive	play	speak	spell

1 Ted can _____ over twenty miles at a time.

2 Lucy can _____ her name in five different languages.

3 Alice can _____ the piano beautifully.

4 Clara can _____ nine different languages.

5 Sandra can _____ a car smoothly.

B   다음 중 어법상 옳은 문장을 있는 대로 고르시오.

① He were able to contact Ms. Lee.

② Helping others can make you happy.

③ We will be able to get there in time.

④ Reading a lot of books can gave you knowledge.

⑤ Most people could understand what he was trying to say.

C   다음 주어진 단어를 이용하여 영작하시오.

1 지하철역에서 값싼 양말을 살 수 있다. (cheap, buy, socks)

  → We can _____ at the subway station.

2 뷔페에서는 원하는 만큼 먹을 수 있다. (you, much, as, eat, as)

  → You can _____ want at the buffet.

3 우리는 함께 영화를 볼 수 있다. (movie, watch, together, the)

  → We can _____.

4 나는 식사 후에는 운동을 할 수 없다. (I, exercise, eat, after)

  → I can't _____.

5 아파서 지금은 너무 크게 말할 수 없다. (too, now, loudly, talk)

  → I can't _____ because I'm sick.

2. 허락의 조동사 can/could/may

A 다음 중 알맞은 단어를 빈칸에 써 넣으시오.

come	go	listen	see	use	

1 May I _____ your phone, please?

2 You can _____ to music in my car.

3 You can _____ to the party if you want.

4 Can I _____ her for a minute?

5 You can _____ with me to the drugstore if you'd like

B 다음 중 어법상 옳은 문장을 있는 대로 고르시오.

① You will may visit the Grand Canyon.

② You cannot sang in this room.

③ Can I help you?

④ We couldn't eat at the fancy restaurant.

⑤ You will be allowed to meet the principal.

C 다음 주어진 단어를 이용하여 영작하시오.

1 개가 더러울 때는 집안으로 들어올 수 없다. (into, when, house, come, the)

→ The dog cannot _____ it's dirty.

2 칠판에 어떤 것이든 써도 된다. (anything, the, write, on)

→ You can _____ chalkboard.

3 원한다면 내 디카를 빌려가도 된다. (digital camera, borrow, my, if)

→ You can _____ you want.

4 내 사무실에서는 그런 말을 쓰면 안 된다. (words, my, use, in, such)

→ You cannot _____ office.

5 내 이메일을 읽어서는 안 된다. (emails, not, my, read)

→ You may _____ _____.

A 다음 중 알맞은 단어를 빈칸에 써 넣으시오.

borrow	give	take	tell	treat

1 Would you let me _____ a few dollars please?

2 Could you _____ me some advice on skiing?

3 Could you _____ me to dinner tonight?

4 Can you _____ me to the hospital right now?

5 Can you _____ my boss that I will not be able to make it to work today?

B 다음 중 어법상 옳은 문장을 있는 대로 고르시오.

① Will you told us about your adventures?

② Would you mind helping me move this box?

③ Could you babysit my cousin for a few days?

④ Can you passed me the paper, please?

⑤ Could you buying some books?

C 다음 주어진 단어를 이용하여 영작하시오.

1 저랑 같이 춤을 춰주실래요? (with, you, dance, can, me)

→ _____?

2 생일 선물로 휴대폰을 사주시겠어요? (for, me, a, buy, cell phone, my)

→ Could you _____ birthday?

3 이 책 좀 읽어주실래요? (to, you, book, can, me, this, read)

→ _____?

4 동생 숙제 좀 도와줄래? (help, her, sister, will, your, with, you)

→ _____ homework?

5 커튼 좀 쳐주시겠어요? (mind, the, would, curtains, drawing, you)

→ _____?

4. 필요·의무의 조동사 must/have to/should/ought to

A 다음 중 알맞은 단어를 빈칸에 써 넣으시오.

ask	drink	finish	go	take

1 I have to _____ water after I take the medicine.

2 We must _____ a break in a few hours.

3 I have to _____ you a few questions before you leave.

4 I have to _____ this work before 6 pm today.

5 My parents have to _____ on a business trip next weekend.

B 다음 중 어법상 옳은 문장을 있는 대로 고르시오.

① We must helped the old lady.

② You ought to see a doctor about the pain in your back.

③ You should be quiet in the study hall.

④ They ought get along with each other.

⑤ A teacher must treat his or her students fairly.

C 다음 주어진 단어를 이용하여 영작하시오.

1 성공하기 위해서는 영어를 배워야만 한다. (in, must, succeed, English, to, you, order, learn)

→ _____ .

2 그들은 집에 머물러 있어야만 했다. (had, home, they, stay, at, to)

→ _____ .

3 그 파티에 갈 필요 없다. (don't, party, have, to, the, you, to, go)

→ _____ .

4 그를 도와서는 안 된다. (not, him, help, you, must)

→ _____ .

5 최선을 다하지 않으면 안 된다. (do, best, must, you, your)

→ _____ .

5. 충고의 조동사 should/ought to/had better

A 다음 중 알맞은 단어를 빈칸에 써 넣으시오.

deal	drive	listen	lose	pay

1 You had better _____ weight.

2 You should not _____ much attention to your appearance.

3 You should _____ with the matter carefully.

4 You ought not to _____ your car fast.

5 They should _____ to their mother.

B 다음 중 어법상 옳은 문장을 있는 대로 고르시오.

① He should take care of his children.

② You had not better follow them.

③ You should stop bothering her.

④ You had better prepare for the entrance exam.

⑤ You ought to not eat too much food.

C 다음 주어진 단어를 이용하여 영작하시오.

1 그녀의 충고를 따라야 한다. (should, her, follow, you, advice)

→ _____.

2 담배를 끊는 편이 낫다. (had, smoking, better, you, stop)

→ _____.

3 좋은 TV 프로그램을 보아야 한다. (TV shows, should, good, you, watch)

→ _____.

4 책을 많이 읽어야 한다. (should, a, you, read, lot)

→ _____.

5 그 파티에는 가지 않는 편이 낫다. (had, go, not, you, to, better)

→ _____ the party.

6. 추측의 조동사 must/can't/may/might

A 다음 중 알맞은 단어를 빈칸에 써 넣으시오.

be	cooking	like	playing	snowing

1 You can't _____ serious.

2 The child must _____ dogs.

3 Brian must be _____ fish.

4 It may be _____ outside.

5 Sandra must be _____ computer games.

B 다음 중 어법상 옳은 문장을 있는 대로 고르시오.

① Willow can't be my boss's daughter.

② They must oversleeping.

③ Next month's trip may be interesting.

④ The strange person maybe right.

⑤ You must be kidding me.

C 다음 주어진 단어를 이용하여 영작하시오.

1 그들은 밖에서 놀고 있음에 틀림없다. (be, outside, must, playing, they)

→ _____ .

2 그 영화는 지루할지도 모른다. (film, be, the, might, boring)

→ _____ .

3 그들은 시간을 허비하고 있음에 틀림없다. (be, time, they, their, must, wasting)

→ _____ .

4 그가 말한 것은 사실일 리가 없다. (be, said, can't, true)

→ What he _____ .

5 그들은 돈을 모으고 있음에 틀림없다. (be, moncy, they, collecting, must)

→ _____ .

A 다음 중 알맞은 단어를 빈칸에 써 넣으시오.

eaten	left	listened	lived	studied

1 Michelle must have _____ in Paris.

2 I should have _____ much harder.

3 You must have _____ before I got there.

4 We should not have _____ so many hamburgers.

5 You shouldn't have _____ to him.

B 다음 중 어법상 옳은 문장을 있는 대로 고르시오.

① They must have being wrong.

② Clara should have paid more attention.

③ Susan may have arrived there.

④ Alice should have drive more carefully.

⑤ It may have rained in the South.

C 다음 주어진 단어를 이용하여 영작하시오.

1 그들이 실수했음에 틀림없다. (have, mistake, they, a, must, made)

→ _____ .

2 그 박물관에 갔어야만 했는데. (have, the, gone, should, to, I, museum)

→ _____ .

3 그녀를 도와주었어야만 했는데. (helped, should, I, her, have)

→ _____ .

4 그 책을 샀어야만 했는데. (should, book, I, bought, the, have)

→ _____ .

5 그녀의 충고를 따랐어야 했는데. (followed, I, her, have, advice, should)

→ _____ .

Chapter 5

부정사

A 다음 중 알맞은 단어를 빈칸에 써 넣으시오.

exercise	go	planned	play	use

1 We chose to _____ chopsticks.

2 To _____ after you eat can be unhealthy.

3 I like to _____ the violin.

4 I _____ to wash my clothes.

5 To _____ out after dark can be very dangerous.

B 다음 중 어법상 옳은 문장을 있는 대로 고르시오.

① Greg continued to work hard.

② He finally decided cleaning up his room.

③ Remember to wash your hands before eating.

④ Susanna loves to play football.

⑤ Eric wants being a writer.

C 다음 주어진 단어를 이용하여 영작하시오.

1 그는 유럽으로 갈 계획이었다. (planned, Europe, go, he, to, to)

→ _____ .

2 그녀는 가수가 되길 바란다. (to, singer, she, a, be, wants)

→ _____ .

3 그들은 우리를 돕기를 거부했다 (to, us, refused, they, help)

→ _____ .

4 그녀는 캐나다로 이주하기로 결심했다. (decided, to, she, to, move, Canada)

→ _____ .

5 그는 문을 잠그는 것을 잊어버렸다. (lock, he, door, forgot, to, the)

→ _____ .

A 다음 중 알맞은 단어를 빈칸에 써 넣으시오.

bake	hate	keep	make	write

1 I need something to _____ with.

2 He has a plan to _____ money.

3 She has a large dog to _____ her company.

4 Most students got to _____ the strict teacher.

5 I know several ways to _____ bread.

B 다음 중 어법상 옳은 문장을 있는 대로 고르시오.

① The teacher seemed to have visit her house.

② Erica seems to be a friendly person.

③ Do you have any wine to give me for?

④ Do you have any plans to get married?

⑤ We need a few lifeguards to watch over the beach.

C 다음 주어진 단어를 이용하여 영작하시오.

1 살 구두가 있나요? (have, buy, you, shoes, do, any, to)

→ _____ .

2 그는 친절한 사람인 것 같다. (seems, person, be, he, kind, to, a)

→ _____ .

3 그녀는 술에 취한 것 같았다. (be, seemed, she, to, drunk)

→ _____ .

4 (글을) 쓸 종이가 좀 필요하다. (need, on, paper, to, some, write, I)

→ _____ .

5 그들은 이미 떠났었던 것 같있다. (seemed, left, have, to, they, already)

→ _____ _____ .

A 다음 중 알맞은 단어를 빈칸에 써 넣으시오.

accept	get	learn	see	win

1 I screamed as loudly as I could to _____ his attention.

2 You were foolish to _____ the offer.

3 They practiced hard to _____ the race.

4 Barbara went to Japan to _____ Japanese.

5 James, I'm glad to _____ you again.

B 다음 중 어법상 옳은 문장을 있는 대로 고르시오.

① My grandfather lived to be eighty.

② They were wise to had chosen the restaurant.

③ Toby studied really hard to pass the examination.

④ The ugly duckling grew up to be a pretty swan.

⑤ Michael was foolish to have drink a beer.

C 다음 주어진 단어를 이용하여 영작하시오.

1 우리는 그녀를 배웅하기 위해 공항으로 갔다. (went, airport, to, to, the, we)

→ _____ see her off.

2 그녀는 자라서 위대한 과학자가 되었다. (up, great, be, she, scientist, grew, a, to)

→ _____ .

3 우리는 그가 살아 있는 것을 보아서 기뻤다. (were, alive, to, we, him, happy, see)

→ _____ .

4 집에 머물러 있었다니 그녀는 현명했다. (was, home, to, she, at, wise, stay)

→ _____ .

5 우리는 영어를 배우기 위해 캐나다로 갔다. (to, English, Canada, went, we, learn, to)

→ _____ .

4. to 부정사 관용 표현

A 다음 중 알맞은 단어를 빈칸에 써 넣으시오. (전치사가 필요한 경우 써 넣으시오.)

begin	build	leave	refuse	understand

1 He was too foolish to _____ what I told him.

2 Michelle was wise enough to _____ to attend the party.

3 They did a lot of things in order to _____ a strong community.

4 She had no choice but to _____ her family.

5 To _____ with, there are a few things you need to know.

B 다음 중 어법상 옳은 문장을 있는 대로 고르시오.

① Her parents were too strict to let her go to the prom.

② Ted was enough foolish to believe what the teacher said.

③ In order to make your dream come true, you ought to do many things.

④ He had no choice but to leave for the United States.

⑤ To frank with you, I did many terrible things.

C 다음 주어진 단어를 이용하여 영작하시오.

1 그는 너무 어려서 말을 탈 수 없다. (too, to, horse, he, ride, is, a, young)

   → _____ .

2 그녀는 친절하게도 나를 안내해주었다. (was, guide, as, kind, she, to, me, so)

   → _____ .

3 행복하게 살기 위해서는, 건강을 유지해야 한다. (live, order, happily, to, in)

   → _____ , you need to stay healthy.

4 그 컴퓨터를 팔지 않을 수 없었다. (no, computer, but, I, sell, had, to, the, choice)

   → _____ .

5 솔직히 말하면, 나는 에리키를 사랑한디. (be, you, Erica, to, with, love, frank, I)

   → _____ .

A 다음 중 알맞은 단어를 빈칸에 써 넣으시오.

| drive | laughing | play | taken | weep |

1 Did you have your picture _____ at the studio?

2 We heard someone _____ the guitar.

3 They couldn't help _____ at their own mistakes.

4 Melissa did nothing but _____.

5 I would rather die than _____ a car.

B 다음 중 어법상 옳은 문장을 있는 대로 고르시오.

① He had his digital camera repaired.

② She heard someone called her name.

③ Can you make yourself understand in Japanese?

④ Barbara had her daughter killed in the crash.

⑤ They couldn't but cry for the child.

C 다음 주어진 단어를 이용하여 영작하시오.

1 그는 누군가가 자기 집에 침입하는 것을 보았다. (into, saw, break, house, he, his, someone)

→ _____ .

2 그녀는 컴퓨터가 수리되도록 했다. (had, repaired, computer, her, she)

→ _____ .

3 우리는 메리가 피아노를 치는 것을 보았다. (Mary, piano, we, play, the, saw)

→ _____ .

4 그는 먹고 자기만 했다. (nothing, sleep, did, and, but, he, eat)

→ _____ .

5 그는 지갑을 도난당했다. (had, stolen, wallet, his, he)

→ _____ .

Chapter 6

동명사

A   다음 주어진 동사를 문맥에 맞게 고치시오.

1   _____ (grow) flowers is fun and fascinating.

2   My hobby is _____ (take) pictures.

3   Joann enjoys _____ (read) historical novels.

4   I'm not used to _____ (use) high-tech machines.

5   Vicky stopped _____ (eat) fast food.

B   다음 중 어법상 옳은 문장을 있는 대로 고르시오.

①   She is used to bake chocolate cookies.

②   He is looking forward to going to Kate's party.

③   Walking fast is good for your health.

④   Steven loves driving a sports car.

⑤   Do not spend money buying such useless stuff.

C   다음 주어진 단어를 이용하여 영작하시오.

1   우리는 아직 숙제를 다 끝내지 못했다. (our, yet, homework, finished)

   → We haven't _____.

2   월요일에는 사무실에서 근무하는 것이 아주 싫다. (office, Mondays, the, working, at, hate, on)

   → I _____.

3   나는 외국에 나가 공부하는 데에 관심이 없다. (studying, interested, not, abroad, in)

   → I'm _____.

4   골프를 치는 것이 테니스를 치는 것보다 더 재미가 있다. (fun, tennis, than, playing, more)

   → Playing golf is _____.

5   외국어를 마스터하는 것은 중요한 일이다. (language, mastering, foreign, a)

   → _____ is important.

2. 동명사의 시제/태

A 다음 주어진 동사를 문맥에 맞게 고치시오.

1 Mike denied _____ (cheat) on his exam.

2 After _____ (complete) the program, he went out for dinner.

3 The boy was ashamed of _____ (scold) in front of other students.

4 We all enjoyed _____ (serve) by the cute waitress.

5 My sister hates _____ (do) her homework.

B 다음 중 어법상 옳은 문장을 있는 대로 고르시오.

① Cloe admitted having broken the window.

② I don't like being treated like a child.

③ He is good at to run and to swim.

④ The girls enjoyed have making cookies.

⑤ He denied being engaged to Paris Hilton.

C 다음 주어진 단어를 이용하여 영작하시오.

1 그녀는 sweetie라고 불리는 것을 싫어했다. (being, sweetie, hated, called)

→ She _____.

2 그는 전에 나를 만났었다는 것을 기억하지 못했다. (before, having, me, met)

→ He didn't remember _____.

3 그들은 초대받지도 않았는데 파티에 참석했다. (invited, without, party, being, the)

→ They attended _____.

4 줄리엣은 지난 한 달 동안 유럽 여행을 했었다고 언급했다.
(month, having, Europe, in, for, a, traveled)

→ Juliet mentioned _____.

5 그는 실수를 저질렀음을 인정했다. (a, made, admitted, mistake, having)

→ He _____.

A 다음 주어진 동사를 문맥에 맞게 고치시오.

1 Do you mind _____ (close) the window?

2 It's raining, but I forgot _____ (bring) the umbrella.

3 He wanted _____ (buy) some fruits.

4 They expected me _____ (play) the main role of the play.

5 Susie regretted _____ (have) made such a choice.

B 다음 중 어법상 옳은 문장을 있는 대로 고르시오.

① Stop nagging me.

② Helen denied to murder the child.

③ I love to cook for my family.

④ The passengers tried to opening the emergency door.

⑤ Ben regretted having rejected the job offer.

C 다음 주어진 단어를 이용하여 영작하시오.

1 그는 여권을 가져오는 것을 잊어버렸다. (forgot, passport, he, his, bring, to)

→ _____.

2 우리는 그 호수에서 수영하는 것을 즐겼다. (enjoyed, lake, swimming, we, the, in)

→ _____.

3 그녀는 보고서를 쓰는 것을 끝마쳤다. (report, finished, she, her, writing)

→ _____.

4 우리는 영어를 완전히 습득하기로 결심했다. (master, we, to, English, decided)

→ _____.

5 우리는 보다 나은 세상을 건설하기를 원한다. (world, to, a, we, better, build, want)

→ _____.

4. 동명사 관용 표현

A 다음 중 알맞은 단어를 빈칸에 써 넣으시오.

> reading   telling   treating   visiting   watching

1 It's no use _____ them to study hard.

2 His latest novel is worth _____.

3 I feel like _____ a horror movie tonight.

4 In _____ a child, be kinder than necessary.

5 She makes a point of _____ the bookstore every day.

B 다음 중 어법상 옳은 문장을 있는 대로 고르시오.

① It's no use helping those lazy people.

② This article is worth reading it.

③ They felt like drank a beer.

④ In pursuing your happiness, you need to choose everything carefully.

⑤ Nicole was on the point of crying.

C 다음 주어진 단어를 이용하여 영작하시오.

1 그에게 충고해 봐야 소용없다. (no, him, advising, It's, use)

→ _____.

2 그녀의 시는 읽을 만한 가치가 있다. (reading, poem, is, her, worth)

→ _____.

3 오늘은 연극을 보고 싶은 생각이 든다. (feel, today, seeing, play, I, a, like)

→ _____.

4 그를 보자마자 그녀는 울음을 터뜨렸다. (seeing, burst, him, she, on, tears, into)

→ _____.

5 그는 막 문을 열려고 했다. (was, door, point, on, of, the, opening, the, he)

→ _____.

Chapter 7

분사

A 다음 주어진 동사를 문맥에 맞게 고치시오.

1 It was _____ (shock) that he stole the money.

2 The lecture was so _____ (confuse) to me.

3 The little girl tried to catch the ball _____ (roll) down the street.

4 Have you ever seen the movie _____ (direct) by Jean-Luc Godard?

5 She looked _____ (surprise) at the result.

B 다음 중 어법상 옳은 문장을 있는 대로 고르시오.

① The man and his dog are run on the riverside.

② She smiled look at her daughter.

③ The baseball had broken the glass.

④ The boy slipped on the recently mopped floor.

⑤ Fallen leaves covered the ground.

C 다음 주어진 단어를 이용하여 영작하시오.

1 지금 누가 방을 청소하고 있니? (right, is, room, now, the, cleaning)

 → Who _____?

2 잠들어 있던 개는 큰 소음에 깨어났다. (dog, awakened, sleeping, was)

 → The _____ by a loud noise.

3 나는 오븐에서 탄 케이크의 냄새를 맡았다. (cake, oven, burnt, the, smelled, in)

 → I _____.

4 필요한 서류를 작성해주십시오. (in, document, fill, required, the)

 → Please _____.

5 내리는 눈이 눈에 보이는 모든 것을 덮었다. (snow, everything, covered, falling)

 → The _____ in sight.

2. 현재분사 vs. 동명사

A 다음 주어진 동사를 문맥에 맞게 고치시오.

1 I am _____ (study) to be a doctor.

2 The _____ (sing) children danced happily.

3 They are _____ (read) the questions on the test.

4 The old man went _____ (fish) to the lake with his grandson.

5 I enjoy _____ (write) a mystery story.

B 다음 중 어법상 옳은 문장을 있는 대로 고르시오.

① Gotten a few questions wrong is not a big deal.

② The rung telephone was picked up by an employee.

③ I got an email written in English.

④ Here are some tips you can try to comfort a crying baby.

⑤ A young soldier was seriously wounded while fighting in Iraq.

C 다음 주어진 단어를 이용하여 영작하시오.

1 아침 식사를 하는 것이 여러 가지 이유에서 좋다. (breakfast, good, eating, is)

→ _____ for many reasons.

2 그는 체조하는 방법을 배우고 있다. (how, gymnastics, learning, to, is, do)

→ He _____.

3 소년들은 호수에 수영하러 갔다. (swimming, the, went, lake, in)

→ The boys _____.

4 나는 문을 열고 있었다. (was, door, I, the, unlocking)

→ _____.

5 그 영화는 무척 감동적이었다. (moving, movie, very, the, was)

→ _____.

A 다음 주어진 동사를 문맥에 맞게 고치시오.

1 In fact, many people are _____ (interest) in learning Japanese.

2 A man _____ (name) Mr. Collins is waiting in the waiting room.

3 Everybody agreed that his new plan was _____ (amaze).

4 I heard someone _____ (scream) upstairs.

5 The weather is _____ (threaten) these days.

B 다음 중 어법상 옳은 문장을 있는 대로 고르시오.

① I saw James taken the taxi the other day.
② This soup was made by my sister.
③ A little girl was trapped inside the burning house.
④ She is knitted a scarf for her mother.
⑤ Kate has finished reading the novel.

C 다음 주어진 단어를 이용하여 영작하시오.

1 할머니께서 꽃밭에 물을 주고 계신다. (flower, watering, the, is, garden)

→ My grandmother _____.

2 그녀는 그 소식에 곤혹스러워하는 것처럼 보였다. (at, looked, news, puzzled, the)

→ She _____.

3 그 교사는 아주 따분한 사람이다. (boring, a, is, person, very)

→ The teacher _____.

4 지난주 발매된 그녀의 새 앨범이 크게 히트했다. (album, released, her, week, new, last)

→ _____ was a big hit.

5 우리는 새로운 식당에서 피자를 먹고 있었다. (the, pizza, new, at, eating, restaurant)

→ We were _____.

4. 분사구문의 형태와 쓰임

A 다음 주어진 동사를 문맥에 맞게 고치시오.

1 _____ (raise) in California, I'm not used to this cold weather.

2 He usually spends a lot of time _____ (work) on the computer.

3 _____ (not, know) where to go, he decided to ask for help.

4 _____ (be) in a hurry, she took a taxi.

5 _____ (satisfy) with the result, the boys shouted for joy.

B 다음 중 어법상 옳은 문장을 있는 대로 고르시오.

① She is in the library studied for her final exam.

② Waiting for someone, she looked out of the window.

③ It being stormy, we had to cancel the outdoor concert.

④ He pulling a large suitcase, he walked to the airport.

⑤ Going straight, you'll find a bookstore.

C 다음 주어진 단어를 이용하여 영작하시오.

1 돈이 없어서 그는 또 점심을 굶었다. (no, having, money)

→ _____, he skipped lunch again.

2 피아노를 배우면서 프레드는 음악을 사랑하기 시작했다. (the, play, to, piano, learning)

→ _____, Fred began to love music.

3 윗옷을 벗고 나서 토니는 의자에 앉았다. (his, off, jacket, taking)

→ _____, Tony sat on a chair.

4 학급 전체를 향해 말하면서, 그는 학생들에게 열심히 공부하라고 말했다.
(class, whole, to, speaking, the)

→ _____, he told his students to study hard.

5 나무에서 구조를 당하고 나서, 그 아이는 한숨을 쉬었다. (from, tree, rescued, the)

→ _____, the child let out a sigh.

Chapter 8

가정법

A   다음 주어진 동사를 이용하여 문맥에 맞게 변형시키시오.

1 If the weather _____ (be) nice, I would go climbing.

2 Rose suggested that we _____ (participate) in the contest.

3 If I _____ (take) the train, I would not be late for work.

4 If she _____ (know) that, she would not have bought a pet.

5 If I _____ (have) a car, I would travel to many places.

B   다음 중 어법상 옳은 문장을 있는 대로 고르시오.

① If that were true, we would be in trouble.

② If I had a bike, I would have gone with him.

③ He insisted that we be polite to others.

④ What would you do if you won a lottery?

⑤ If there are nothing to do, I would go shopping with you.

C   다음 주어진 단어를 이용하여 영작하시오.

1 내가 너라면 그런 책을 읽지 않을 텐데. (would, such, book, read, a, not)

→ If I were you, I _____.

2 네가 내 충고를 받아들였다면, 그런 실수는 하지 않았을 텐데.
(have, a, made, you, such, not, mistake, would)

→ If you had taken my advice, _____.

3 우리가 표를 미리 사뒀더라면 오랫동안 기다리지 않았을 텐데.
(waited, not, long, have, would, so)

→ If we had bought the tickets in advance, we _____.

_____

2. 가정법 과거

A 다음 주어진 동사를 문맥에 맞게 고치시오.

1 If I _____ (have) some time, I would go to her wedding.

2 If he _____ (be) here now, he would help me with this.

3 If you _____ (join) the club, he would be very happy.

4 If they visited me, we would _____ (go) to the soccer game together.

5 If it didn't rain so hard, we would _____ (take) the airplane as scheduled.

B 다음 중 어법상 옳은 문장을 있는 대로 고르시오.

① You knew the answer if you listened carefully in class.

② If you helped me, I would buy you lunch.

③ If it were colder, it would snow.

④ If Tommy knew that I broke his bike, he will be very upset.

⑤ If I were a bird, I could fly to you.

C 다음 주어진 단어를 이용하여 영작하시오.

1 날씨가 좋으면 낚시를 갈 텐데.

(were, go, the, we, fine, fishing, weather, would)

→ If _____ .

2 사무실에 자판기가 있다면 우리에게 도움이 될 텐데.

(vending, help, there, office, a, the, were, us, that, machine, in, would)

→ If _____ .

3 그녀가 채식주의자가 아니라면 그녀와 그 식당에 갈 텐데.

(to, vegetarian, restaurant, her, she, a, the, would, not, were, go, with, I)

→ If _____ .

A 다음 주어진 동사를 문맥에 맞게 고치시오.

1 If you _____ (not, go) to bed so late, you wouldn't have missed your plane.

2 If she had come with me, I _____ (not, be) so lonely.

3 If we had arrived there earlier, we _____ (meet) him in person.

4 If he _____ (study) English harder, he could have gotten the job.

5 If it _____ (be, not) a national holiday, we would have been in school.

B 다음 중 어법상 옳은 문장을 있는 대로 고르시오.

① If it had rained hard, what will you do?

② If you had turned on the heat, it wouldn't have been so cold.

③ If Sam didn't reminded me to get gas, I would have forgotten to do it.

④ If I had been you, I wouldn't have bought such an expensive scarf.

⑤ If Tim had angered his boss, he would have been fired.

C 다음 주어진 단어를 이용하여 영작하시오.

1 그녀가 지갑을 잃어버렸다면, 울었을 텐데.

(had, wallet, cried, she, she, her, have, lost, would)

→ If _____.

2 그렇게 많이 먹지 않았다면 아프지 않았을 텐데.

(eaten, been, would, have, had, not, not, so, you, you, much, sick)

→ If _____.

3 더 열심히 일했다면 돈을 더 많이 벌었을 텐데

(worked, made, harder, I, I, had, have, money, would, more)

→ If _____.

4. as if / I wish 가정법

A 다음 두 문장의 뜻이 같아지도록 주어진 동사를 문맥에 맞게 고치시오.

1 I wish you _____ (be) here.

= I'm sorry that you are not here.

2 I wish you _____ (get) me something to drink.

= I'm sorry you didn't get me something to drink.

3 Ross acts as if he _____ (write) the article himself.

= In fact, Ross didn't write the article himself.

B 다음 중 어법상 옳은 문장을 있는 대로 고르시오.

① I wish he has come with me.
② He acted as if he were rich.
③ The guy spoke as if he were a lawyer.
④ I wished I live a different life.
⑤ She talked as if she will travel all over the world.

C 다음 주어진 단어를 이용하여 영작하시오.

1 나에게 강아지가 한 마리 있다면 좋을 텐데. (a, had, dog, I, wish)

→ I _____.

2 내가 일본어를 잘할 수 있으면 좋을 텐데. (spoke, wish, I, well, Japanese)

→ I _____.

3 그녀는 마치 자신이 백만장자인 것처럼 얘기한다. (a, if, were, millionaire, as, she)

→ She talks _____.

4 그는 마치 자신이 내 남자친구인 것처럼 행동한다. (as, acts, my, were, he, boyfriend, if)

→ He _____.

5 그녀는 마치 자신이 전문가인 것처럼 말한다. (expert, if, were, speaks, an, as, she)

→ She _____.

Chapter 9

일치와 화법

A 다음 주어진 동사를 문맥에 맞게 고치시오.

1 Both Sarah and her brother _____ (like) apples.

2 One of my colleagues _____ (be) from Cuba.

3 Thirty miles _____ (be) a long distance.

4 Every student and parent who _____ (want) to come is welcome.

5 The man and his son _____ (run) the company.

B 다음 중 어법상 옳은 문장을 있는 대로 고르시오.

① Neither this nor that are good.

② Most of the work have not been completed yet.

③ Each of the members has to prepare his or her food.

④ The students as well as the teacher do not like the idea.

⑤ The glasses on the table is my father's.

C 다음 주어진 단어를 이용하여 영작하시오.

1 우리들 중 한 명은 집을 지켜야 한다.

   (after, of, has, look, to, one, us)

   → _____ the house.

2 당신이나 그 사람 중에 한 명은 운전해야 합니다.

   (has, either, or, to, you, he)

   → _____ drive a car.

3 그와 그의 부인은 둘 다 아이를 입양하고 싶어 한다.

   (and, to, his, he, child, both, a, adopt, wife, want)

   → _____.

2. 시제 일치

A 다음 주어진 동사를 문맥에 맞게 고치시오

1 Columbus proved that the earth _____ (be) round.

2 I _____ (fall) asleep because I had nothing to do.

3 I know that my coworker _____ (major) in computer science in college.

4 He said that President John F. Kennedy _____ (be) killed in 1963.

5 These are the pictures of the people who really _____ (build) this pyramid.

B 다음 중 어법상 옳은 문장을 있는 대로 고르시오.

① Yesterday, I bought four apples and ate them all.

② The book says an ostrich was the largest living bird in the world.

③ Our science teacher said that a star is just a big ball of gas.

④ We know that you told a lie to us.

⑤ Did you hear that one of the boys gets hurt from the accident?

C 다음 주어진 단어를 이용하여 영작하시오.

1 우리는 모두 네가 최선을 다했다고 생각해.

(believed, did, you, we, your, that, best)

→ _____ .

2 나는 프랑스어가 캐나다의 공용어라는 것을 몰랐다.

(language, Canada, official, French, an, is, of)

→ I didn't know that _____ .

3 과학 선생님은 물이 산소와 수소로 구성되어 있다고 말했다.

(oxygen, hydrogen, science, water, said, our, consists, of, teacher, and, that)

→ _____ .

A 직접화법을 간접화법으로 바꿀 때 빈칸에 적절한 말을 쓰시오.

1 "I'll see the doctor," Bob said.

= Bob said that he _____ the doctor.

2 Ann said, "I lived in Ilsan."

= Ann said that she _____ in Ilsan.

3 She said to me, "I know your sister."

= She _____ me that she knew my sister.

B 다음 중 어법상 옳은 문장을 있는 대로 고르시오.

① My friend said that he loses his new camera.

② The girl said, "Mommy, I'd like to have a cat."

③ Billy said it has taken one hour for him to reach the workplace.

④ Chris said she had eaten three cupcakes in one hour.

⑤ The old man said that the pen is mightier than the sword.

C 다음 주어진 단어를 이용하여 영작하시오.

1 그녀는 자기에게 좋은 계획이 있다고 말했다.

(plan, a, me, had, great, that, told, she, she)

→ _____.

2 그녀는 한때 자신의 취미가 영어로 일기를 쓰는 것이었다고 한다..

(hobby, stamps, says, used, collecting, she, her, be, that, to)

→ _____.

3 Adams는 지구가 태양 주위를 돈다고 말했다.

(the, the, that, Adams, moves, sun, said, around, earth)

→ _____.

4. 의문문의 화법 전환

A 다음 주어진 동사(구)를 문맥에 맞게 고치시오.

1 My doctor asked me if I _____ (have suffer) from insomnia.

2 Lucy asked me why I _____ (have lie) to her.

3 Thomas asked me how I _____ (have solve) the problem.

4 Lewis asked me if I _____ (want) a strawberry cake for dessert.

5 She asked me whether the mailman _____ (have come).

B 다음 중 어법상 옳은 문장을 있는 대로 고르시오.

① She asked me what she had to do.

② They asked her if does she agree.

③ He asked me that I could let him borrow my car.

④ The professor asked us if we had any questions.

⑤ Susie asked me whether I would make it to the party or not.

C 다음 주어진 단어를 이용하여 영작하시오.

1 선생님은 우리에게 선생님이 한 말을 이해했는지 물었다.

(asked, the, understood, we, us, said, he, what, if, teacher)

→ _____ .

2 그는 내가 스페인에서 얼마나 머물 것인지 물었다.

(stay, long, he, me, asked, Spain, how, in, would, I)

→ _____ .

3 그녀는 내게 돈을 빌려줄 수 있느냐고 물었다.

(if, her, she, I, money, asked, lend, me, could)

→ _____ .

A   다음 주어진 동사(구)를 문맥에 맞게 고치시오.

1   Our teacher said to us, "Don't forget to do your homework."

= Our teacher told us _____ to do our homework.

2   I said to him, "Let's go out for dinner."

= I suggested to him that we _____ out for dinner.

3   The professor said to us, "Take notes."

= The professor told us _____ notes.

B   다음 중 어법상 옳은 문장을 있는 대로 고르시오.

① My neighbor warned me to not play the piano at night.

② He reminded me to paint the fence.

③ The police ordered everyone to leave the place.

④ Mom told me to ordered a pizza and a bottle of coke.

⑤ Jimmy told me turning down the volume.

C   다음 주어진 단어를 이용하여 영작하시오.

1   상사가 내게 다시는 지각하지 말라고 경고했다.

(warned, late, be, not, boss, me, my, to, again)

→ _____ .

2   코치가 내게 체중을 줄이라고 충고했다.

(lose, advised, me, my, weight, to, coach)

→ _____ .

3   남자친구가 콘서트에 가자고 제안했다.

(suggested, go, boyfriend, concert, we, my, a, to, that)

→ _____ .

TOP GRAMMAR

For Intermediate
Students - 1

Workbook

TOP GRAMMAR

중급 - 1
For Intermediate Students

GRAMMAR

정답 및 해설

WorldCom

Top Grammar
중급-1

정답 및 해설

unit 01 자동사 vs. 타동사
p.11

EXERCISES

A

1 raise   2 rises   3 felled
4 fell   5 laid   6 lay
7 waited

B

1 T
2 F, went → went to
3 F, married with → married
4 F, reached to → reached
5 T
6 F, wait → wait for
7 F, complained → complained of

C

③ laughs → laughs at

Workbook

A

1 apologized   2 join   3 agree
4 resembles   5 marry

B

②, ④

C

1 affects your body in many ways
2 complains about something
3 in the room opposed my suggestion
4 take care of my younger sister
5 went out to attend the meeting

unit 02 완전동사 vs. 불완전동사
p.13

EXERCISES

A

1 beautiful   2 traitor   3 terrible
4 great   5 silent   6 mad
7 strange

B

1 F, angrily → angry
2 F, calmly → calm
3 T
4 F, freshly → fresh
5 T
6 F, sadly → sad
7 T

C

③ madly → mad

Workbook

A

1 lonely [보]
2 pilot [보]
3 e-mails [목]
4 political problems [목]
5 better [보]

B

①, ②, ④

C

1 looked very young for her age
2 answered my question
3 turned red at his remark
4 cooked dinner for us
5 bought a big suitcase yesterday

unit 03 수여동사
p.15

EXERCISES

A

1 for	2 to	3 to
4 for	5 of	
6 for	7 to	

B

1 F, of → to
2 T
3 F, to → of
4 F, of → to
5 T
6 F, of → for
7 T

C

③ of → to

Workbook

A

1 X	2 for	3 of
4 to	5 to	

B

②, ③, ⑤

C

1 gave her wedding ring to me
2 bought a book for his girlfriend
3 give me your phone number
4 teaches me English
5 send this package to

unit 04 불완전타동사
p.17

EXERCISES

A

1 fixed	2 to lend	3 to get
4 blow	5 go	
6 arrested	7 study	

B

1 F, called → to call
2 T
3 F, stolen → steal
4 F, doing → done
5 T
6 F, to feel → feel
7 T

C

⑤ to become → become

Workbook

A

1 to become	2 hold(ing)
3 to go	4 understand
5 get	

B

①, ②, ⑤

C

1 had the fence painted white
2 did not hear the baby cry
3 asked me to take care of her cat
4 you to take this position
5 a way to make people laugh

Chapter Review

A

1 wept → wept at
  - weep이 자동사이기 때문에 그 다음에 명사를 쓸 때는 대개 전치사가 필요하다.

2 married with → married
  - marry가 타동사이기 때문에 목적어가 바로 와야 하며 with과 함께 쓸 수 없다.

3 entered into → entered
  - enter가 타동사이기 때문에 목적어가 바로 와야 하며 into와 함께 쓸 수 없다.

4 discuss about → discuss
  - discuss가 타동사이기 때문에 목적어가 바로 와야 하며 about과 함께 쓸 수 없다.

5 complained → complained of
  - complain이 자동사이기 때문에 목적어가 오려면 전치사 of가 있어야 한다.

6 reached to → reached
  - reach가 타동사이기 때문에 목적어가 바로 와야 하며 to와 함께 쓸 수 없다.

7 To our surprise, the loser looked happily.

8 quietly → quiet
  - 부사는 원칙적으로 be동사의 보어로 쓰일 수 없다.

9 toughly → tough
  - toughly와 같은 부사는 원칙적으로 불완전자동사의 보어로 쓰일 수 없다.

10 angrily → angry
  - angrily와 같은 부사는 원칙적으로 불완전자동사의 보어로 쓰일 수 없다.

11 happily → happy
  - happily와 같은 부사는 원칙적으로 불완전자동사의 보어로 쓰일 수 없다.

12 sourly → sour
  - sourly와 같은 부사는 원칙적으로 불완전자동사의 보어로 쓰일 수 없다.

13 for → to
  - sell은 문형 전환에서 전치사로 to를 쓰는 수여동사이다.

14 to → for
  - buy는 문형 전환에서 전치사로 for를 쓰는 수여동사이다.

15 of → for
  - make은 문형 전환에서 전치사로 for를 쓰는 수여동사이다.

16 to → for
  - save는 문형 전환에서 전치사로 for를 쓰는 수여동사이다.

17 to → of
  - ask는 문형 전환에서 전치사로 of를 쓰는 수여동사이다.

18 of → to
  - give는 문형 전환에서 전치사로 to를 쓰는 수여동사이다.

19 of → to
  - send는 문형 전환에서 전치사로 to를 쓰는 수여동사이다.

20 help → to help
  - ask의 목적격보어로는 to부정사가 와야 한다.

21 to pierce → pierced
  - 사역동사 have의 목적격보어인데 수동의 관계이므로 과거분사가 와야 한다.

22 to darken → darken(ing)
  - 지각동사 watch의 목적격보어이므로 원형부정사나 현재분사가 와야 한다.

23 to change → change [changing]
  - 지각동사 have의 목적격보어이므로 원형부정사나 현재분사가 와야 한다.

24 to go → go
  - 사역동사 let의 목적격보어이므로 원형부정사가 와야 한다.

25 to beat → beat(ing)
  - 지각동사 feel의 목적격보어이므로 원형부정사나 현재분사가 와야 한다.

B

⑤

C

④ to say → say

D

1 b	2 d	3 b
4 d	5 c	6 d
7 c	8 b	9 d
10 b	11 c	12 a
13 b	14 d	15 c
16 c	17 d	18 b
19 d	20 c	

Chapter 2 _ 시제

unit 01 현재시제
p.25

EXERCISES

A

1 boils　　　　2 ends　　　3 marry
4 travel　　　 5 miss　　　6 visit
7 find

B

1 F, live → lived
2 T
3 T
4 F, will leave → leave
5 F, came → comes
6 F, will know → know
7 T

C

③ will be → are

Workbook

A

1 freezes　　　2 is　　　3 goes
4 want　　　　5 have

B

②, ③, ④

C

1 The last bus leaves at 11:40 p.m.
2 want to be an astronaut
3 drinks a glass of milk every morning
4 consists of hydrogen and oxygen
5 goes to a ski resort every winter

unit 02 과거시제
p.27

EXERCISES

A

1 visit　　　　2 spoke　　3 cost
4 hanged　　　5 laid
6 used to　　　7 invaded

B

1 F, beated → beat
2 T
3 F, laid → lay
4 F, mistaked → mistook
5 T
6 F, has started → started
7 T

C

④ has taught → taught

Workbook

A

1 majored　　　2 snowed
3 traveled　　　4 invented
5 got

B

①, ②, ④

C

1 bought a notebook computer yesterday
2 wrote a novel last year
3 decided to go on a diet
4 asked her about her new work
5 moved here ten years ago

EXERCISES

A

1 will
2 visit
3 will rain
4 will
5 are going to
6 will come
7 don't

B

1 T
2 T
3 F, will see → sees
4 F, wins → will win
5 F, won't attend → doesn't attend
6 T
7 T

C

② will get → get

Workbook

A

1 will feel
2 is going to rain
3 will tell
4 will treat
5 are going to have

B

②, ③, ⑤

C

1 will stay in Boston one more year
2 will not do the work by myself
3 It will be hot and humid tomorrow.
4 If you find the answer
5 He will go to Canada.

EXERCISES

A

1 talked
2 called
3 walked
4 eaten
5 has loved
6 sent
7 climbed

B

1 T
2 F, ago → before
3 F, were → have been
4 T
5 F, have thrown → threw
6 F, hated → has hated
7 T

C

② has ended → ended

Workbook

A

1 finished
2 have you stayed
3 has been
4 have not read
5 went

B

②, ③

C

1 have been to New York
2 has not eaten at all
3 worked on the project for three weeks
4 have not met him for ten years
5 have finished reading the book

EXERCISES

A

1	had	2	had	3	had
4	had	5	have		
6	have	7	have		

B

1 F, has put → had put
2 T
3 F, will have eaten → had eaten
4 T
5 F, will had discovered → will have discovered
6 T
7 T

C

⑤ will have saved → had saved

Workbook

A

1 had lived   2 had finished
3 had never met   4 will have ended
5 had learned

B

②, ③, ⑤

C

1 had already left the office
2 She had read a book
3 I had used a digital camera.
4 will have worked for this company for thirty years
5 had never been abroad

EXERCISES

A

1	is reading	2	hate
3	resembles	4	belongs
5	own	6	does not understand
7	do not exist		

B

1 T
2 F, are wanting → want
3 T
4 F, am having → have
5 F, is seeming → seems
6 F, are disliking → dislike
7 T

C

② am loving → love

Workbook

A

1 mopping   2 cooking
3 was doing   4 belongs
5 do not understand

B

①, ②, ③

C

1 was watching a horror movie
2 They were having lunch.
3 He was driving a truck.
4 The new teacher seems nice.
5 I was sleeping at home.

Chapter Review

A

1 go → went
- yesterday라는 분명히 과거를 나타내는 말이 있기 때문에 과거시제를 써야 한다.

2 boiled → boils
- 변하지 않는 과학적 사실은 현재시제로 나타낸다.

3 will finish → finish
- 시간의 부사절에서는 미래시제가 아니라 현재시제를 써야 한다.

4 will come → comes
- 조건의 부사절에서는 미래시제가 아니라 현재시제를 써야 한다.

5 has given → gave
- yesterday라는 분명히 과거를 나타내는 말이 있기 때문에 과거시제를 써야 한다.

6 has broken → broke
- 역사적 사실이므로 과거로 나타내야 한다.

7 digged → dug
- dig의 과거형은 dug이다.

8 lied → laid
- "알을 낳다"는 뜻의 타동사 lay의 과거형은 laid 이다.

9 am going to → will
- 바로 결정한 경우이기 때문에 will이 자연스럽다.

10 will fail → fail
- 조건의 부사절에서는 현재시제가 미래시제를 대신한다.

11 came → will come
- if가 명사절을 이끌고 있기 때문에 미래시제가 가능하다.

12 will end → ends
- 조건의 부사절에서는 현재시제가 미래시제를 대신한다.

13 have walked → walked
- yesterday라는 분명히 과거를 나타내는 말이 있기 때문 과거시제를 써야 한다.

14 ago → before
- ago는 과거시제와 어울리지 현재완료와는 어울릴 수 없다.

15 learned → have learned
- since의 앞에 오는 절은 현재완료를 써야 한다.

16 has finished → finished
- just now라는 분명히 과거를 나타내는 말이 있기 때문에 과거시제를 써야 한다.

17 have met → met
- last weekend라는 분명히 과거를 나타내는 말이 있기 때문에 과거시제를 써야 한다.

18 will have → had
- 과거의 일정한 시점 이전에 일어난 일이므로 과거 완료를 써야 한다.

19 graduate → graduated
- 미래완료는 「will have+과거분사」라는 형태로 써야 한다.

10 will have visit → had visited
- 과거의 일정한 시점 이전에 일어난 일이므로 과거 완료를 써야 한다.

21 had → have
- 미래완료는 「will have+과거분사」라는 형태로 써야 한다.

22 am knowing → know
- know는 진행형으로 쓸 수 없는 동사이다.

23 swim → swimming
- 현재진행형은 「am [are, is]+ -ing」라는 형태로 써야 한다.

24 is belonging → belongs
- belong은 진행형으로 쓸 수 없는 동사이다.

25 is having → has
- have는 진행형으로 쓸 수 없는 동사이다.

B
⑤

C
③ won't be → aren't

D

1 b	2 c	3 d
4 c	5 d	6 a
7 b	8 c	9 b
10 b	11 c	12 b
13 d	14 b	15 d
16 d	17 b	18 d
19 a	20 b	

Chapter 3 _ 태

unit 01 수동태의 기본 형식
p.43

EXERCISES

A

1 turned 2 worn 3 polluted
4 stolen 5 treated
6 roasted 7 sold

B

1 F, invite → invited
2 F, win → won
3 T
4 T
5 F, treat → treated
6 F, wrote → written
7 F, lead → led

C

③ give → given

Workbook

A

1 made 2 hit
3 transferred 4 sung
5 reelected

B

①, ③, ⑤

C

1 were pleased to hear the news
2 was painted by my husband
3 was decorated in green and white
4 was made by a Japanese craftsman
5 was attacked by teenage hackers last week

unit 02 4형식 문형의 수동태
p.45

EXERCISES

A

1 to 2 given 3 to
4 for 5 asked
6 to 7 taught

B

1 F, give → given
2 T
3 F, show → shown
4 T
5 F, to 삭제
6 F, make → made
7 F, to 삭제

C

③ to 삭제

Workbook

A

1 to 2 to 3 to
4 for 5 to

B

①, ②

C

1 was sent to my uncle
2 was given to his daughter
3 was bought for Jane
4 were taught math by Mary
5 was asked a hard question

EXERCISES

A

1 to be   2 to be
3 to overwork   4 to play
5 to be   6 to sell
7 playing

B

1 T
2 F, take → to take
3 T
4 F, win → to win
5 T
6 T
7 F, play → playing [to play]

C

② give → to give

Workbook

A

1 Jacob
2 to join
3 peeping

B

③, ④, ⑤

C

1 was elected president of my class
2 were made to wear school uniforms
3 was seen to break into the store
4 was considered an excellent writer
5 was believed to cure lung cancer

EXERCISES

A

1 have   2 being   3 been
4 being   5 been
6 being   7 been

B

1 T
2 F, had → have
3 T
4 F, being → been
5 T
6 F, been → being
7 F, spill → spilled [spilt]

C

① been → being

Workbook

A

1 is being played
2 will have been constructed
3 has been solved
4 had been directed
5 was being used

B

①, ②

C

1 was being built
2 was being tied to the post
3 is being dug by three boys
4 has been heated
5 has been reviewed by the critics

unit 05   수동태 관용 표현
p.51

EXERCISES

A

1 with	2 with	3 at
4 with	5 in	6 of
7 about		

B

1 F, fill → filled
2 F, of → with [at]
3 T
4 F, of → with
5 F, interesting → interested
6 T
7 F, with → about

C

⑤ concerned of → concerned about

Workbook

A

1 filled	2 disappointed
3 interested	4 amazed
5 frightened	

B

②, ③, ④

C

1 satisfied with your job
2 is covered with white tiles
3 is well-known to many people
4 was worried about his presentation
5 are interested in his research

Chapter Review

A

1 see → seen
   ▪ 수동태이므로 『be 동사+과거분사』형태로 써야
     한다.

2 from → of
   ▪ rob A of B가 수동태로 바뀐 형태인데, B앞의 전
     치사는 of를 그대로 써야 한다.

3 steal → stolen
   ▪ 수동태이므로 『be 동사+과거분사』형태로 써야
     한다.

4 of → to
   ▪ 4형식의 수동태인데, sell은 전치사로 to를 쓰는
     대표적인 동사이다.

5 wore → worn
   ▪ 수동태이므로 『be 동사+과거분사』형태로 써야
     한다.

6 to 삭제
   ▪ 4형식의 수동태인데, 간접목적어가 주어로 쓰였기
     때문에 전치사가 필요 없다.

7 of → for
   ▪ 4형식의 수동태인데, buy는 전치사로 for를 쓰는
     대표적인 동사이다.

8 of 삭제
   ▪ 4형식의 수동태인데, 간접목적어가 주어로 쓰였기
     때문에 전치사가 필요 없다.

9 of → to
   ▪ 4형식의 수동태인데, show는 전치사로 to를 쓰는
     대표적인 동사이다.

10 to → for
   ▪ 4형식의 수동태인데, cook은 전치사로 for를 쓰는
     대표적인 동사이다.

11 arrive → to arrive
   ▪ 5형식의 수동태인데, expected 다음에는 반드시
     to부정사가 와야 한다.

12 build → to build
   ▪ 5형식의 수동태인데, made 다음에는 반드시
     to부정사가 와야 한다.

13 break → breaking [to break]
   ▪ 5형식의 수동태에서는 지각동사 다음에 to부정사
     나 현재분사가 와야 한다.

14 be → to be
   ▪ 5형식의 수동태인데, considered 다음에는 반드
     시 to부정사가 와야 한다.

15 sing → singing [to sing]
   ▪ 5형식의 수동태에서는 지각동사 다음에 to부정사
     나 현재분사가 와야 한다.

16 been → being
- 진행형 수동태이므로 been이 아니라 being을 써야 한다.

17 being → been
- 완료형 수동태이므로 being이 아니라 been을 써야 한다.

18 using → used
- 완료형 수동태이므로 been 다음에 과거분사가 와야 한다.

19 being → been
- 완료형 수동태이므로 being이 아니라 been을 써야 한다.

20 took → taken
- 진행형 수동태이므로 being 다음에 과거분사가 와야 한다.

21 about → with
- filled 다음에 오는 전치사는 with이다.

22 delight → delighted
- 수동태 형식이므로 동사원형이 아니라 과거분사를 써야 한다.

23 interesting → interested
- 수동태 형식이므로 현재분사가 아니라 과거분사를 써야 한다.

24 with → of [at]
- frightened 다음에 오는 전치사는 of나 at이다.

25 at → about
- "우려하는"이란 뜻의 concerned 다음에 오는 전치사는 about이다.

B
③

C
② surprising → surprised

D

1 d	2 c	3 a
4 b	5 d	6 b
7 d	8 c	9 d
10 c	11 b	12 d
13 c	14 b	15 d
16 c	17 d	18 b
19 d	20 b	

---

unit 01 가능·능력의 조동사 can/could/may
p.59

EXERCISES

A
1	shoot	2	understand
3	can	4	be
5	play	6	to attend
7	will be able to		

B
1 T
2 F, played → play
3 F, seeing → see
4 F, been → be
5 F, playing → play
6 T
7 F, can may → may

C
② survived → survive

Workbook

A
1 bike	2 spell	3 play
4 speak	5 drive	

B
②, ③, ⑤

C
1 buy cheap socks
2 eat as much as you
3 watch the movie together
4 exercise after I eat
5 talk too loudly now

unit 02　허락의 조동사 can/could/may
p.61

EXERCISES

A

1 talk　　2 have　　3 enter
4 trespass　5 go　　6 say
7 play

B

1 T
2 F, drank → drink
3 F, riding → ride
4 F, takes → take
5 F, had → have
6 T
7 F, can will → will be able to

C

② pursued → pursue

Workbook

A

1 use　　2 listen　　3 go
4 see　　5 come

B

③, ④, ⑤

C

1 come into the house when
2 write anything on the
3 borrow my digital camera if
4 use such words in my
5 not read my emails

unit 03　요청의 조동사 will/can/would/could
p.63

EXERCISES

A

1 do　　2 take　　3 pass
4 opening　5 buy
6 reply　　7 lending

B

1 T
2 F, taking → take
3 F, sent → send
4 F, to help → helping
5 F, stayed → stay
6 F, given → give
7 T

C

② to help → helping

Workbook

A

1 borrow　　2 give　　3 treat
4 take　　5 tell

B

②, ③

C

1 Can you dance with me?
2 buy me a cell phone for my
3 Can you read this book to me?
4 Will you help your sister with her
5 Would you mind drawing the curtains?

unit 04 필요·의무의 조동사 must/have to/ should/ought to

p.65

EXERCISES

A

1	had to	2	has	3	have
4	don't	5	have	6	to take
7	think				

B

1 T
2 F, have to → has to
3 F, ought come → ought to come
4 T
5 F, should to → should
6 F, stretched → stretch
7 T

C

⑤ must to → must

Workbook

A

1	drink	2	take	3	ask
4	finish	5	go		

B

②, ③, ⑤

C

1 In order to succeed, you must learn English.
2 They had to stay at home.
3 You don't have to go to the party.
4 You must not help him.
5 You must do your best.

unit 05 충고의 조동사 should/ought to/ had better

p.67

EXERCISES

A

1	had	2	should	
3	use	4	to get	
5	not to	6	better not	
7	wear			

B

1 T
2 F, had not better → had better not
3 F, ought leave → ought to leave
4 F, ought to not → ought not to
5 F, have better → had better
6 T
7 F, use to → to use

C

③ ought not look → ought not to look

Workbook

A

1	lose	2	pay	3	deal
4	drive	5	listen		

B

①, ③, ④

C

1 You should follow her advice.
2 You had better stop smoking.
3 You should watch good TV shows.
4 You should read a lot.
5 You had better not go to

unit 06 추측의 조동사 must/can't/may/might
p.69

EXERCISES

A

1	be	2	can't	3	may be
4	must	5	can't	6	must
7	can't				

B

1 T
2 F, must not → can't[cannot]
3 F, can be not → cannot[can't] be
4 T
5 F, may taking → may take
6 F, must not be → can't[cannot] be
7 T

C

④ maybe → may be

Workbook

A

1	be	2	like	3	cooking
4	snowing	5	playing			

B

①, ③, ⑤

C

1 They must be playing outside.
2 The film might be boring.
3 They must be wasting their time.
4 said can't be true
5 They must be collecting money.

unit 07 조동사＋have＋과거분사
p.71

EXERCISES

A

1	must	2	touched	3	have
4	passed	5	must	6	should
7	must				

B

1 T
2 F, should had bought → should have bought
3 T
4 T
5 F, must have fix → must have fixed
6 F, should has known → should have known
7 T

C

⑤ must have → should have

Workbook

A

1	lived	2	studied	3	left
4	eaten	5	listened			

B

②, ③, ⑤

C

1 They must have made a mistake.
2 I should have gone to the museum.
3 I should have helped her.
4 I should have bought the book.
5 I should have followed her advice.

Chapter Review

A

1 can may → can
- 조동사끼리 결합하여 쓸 수 없다.

2 able reopen → able to reopen
- able 다음에는 to부정사가 와야 한다.

3 could able → were able
- could 대신 쓸 수 있는 표현은 were[was] able to이다.

4 played → play
- 조동사 다음에는 동사 원형이 와야 한다.

5 will may → may
- 조동사끼리 결합하여 쓸 수 없다.

6 allow → allowed
- may를 대신할 수 있는 표현은 be allowed to 이다.

7 Must → Can
- 간단한 요청이기 때문에 can을 써야 한다.

8 Should → Can [Would, Could]
- 요청이기 때문에 can, could, would 등을 써야 한다.

9 to give → giving
- mind 다음에는 반드시 동명사가 와야 한다.

10 have → has
- 3인칭 단수 현재형 다음에는 have to가 아니라 has to를 써야 한다.

11 help → to help
- ought 다음에는 반드시 to부정사가 와야 한다.

12 must should → should [must]
- 조동사끼리 결합하여 쓸 수 없다.

13 musted → had to
- must는 과거형이 없으므로 had to로 표현해야 한다.

14 have better → had better
- 충고를 나타내는 조동사는 had better이다.

15 wear → to wear
- ought 다음에는 반드시 to부정사가 와야 한다.

16 should must → should
- 조동사끼리 결합하여 쓸 수 없다.

17 going → go
- had better 다음에는 동사 원형이 와야 한다.

18 must can → must [can't]
- 조동사끼리 결합하여 쓸 수 없다.

19 maybe → may be
- "~일지도 모른다"는 표현이므로 "may be"로 나타내야 한다.

20 must should → must
- 조동사끼리 결합하여 쓸 수 없다.

21 must not → cannot [can't]
- 강한 부정의 추측이기 때문에 cannot을 써야 한다.

22 leave → left
- 「must have + 과거분사」의 형태로 써야 한다.

23 having → have
- 「should have + 과거분사」의 형태로 써야 한다.

24 had → have
- 「must have + 과거분사」의 형태로 써야 한다.

25 went → gone
- 「should have + 과거분사」의 형태로 써야 한다.

B

④

C

④ had better → may

D

1 c	2 b	3 a
4 c	5 b	6 b
7 d	8 b	9 d
10 a	11 d	12 b
13 d	14 b	15 c
16 b	17 d	18 b
19 c	20 d	

Chapter 5 _ 부정사

unit 01 명사적 용법
p.79

EXERCISES

A

1 to understand   2 to read
3 to bring   4 to engage
5 to listen   6 to dress
7 to become

B

1 T
2 F, go → go to
3 F, watched → watching [to watch]
4 F, visiting → to visit
5 F, to playing → to play
6 T
7 F, fixes → to fix

C

⑤ being → to be

Workbook

A

1 use   2 exercise   3 play
4 planned   5 go

B

①, ③, ④

C

1 He planned to go to Europe.
2 She wants to be a singer.
3 They refused to help us.
4 She decided to move to Canada.
5 He forgot to lock the door.

unit 02 형용사적 용법
p.81

EXERCISES

A

1 to take   2 to open
3 to provide   4 be performed
5 familiar   6 feel
7 to hate

B

1 F, to write → to write on
2 T
3 F, guarded → to guard
4 F, to had made → to have made
5 T
6 F, to happy → happy [to be happy]
7 F, disliked → to dislike

C

④ to be confuse → to be confused

Workbook

A

1 write   2 make   3 keep
4 hate   5 bake

B

②, ④, ⑤

C

1 Do you have any shoes to buy?
2 He seems to be a kind person.
3 She seemed to be drunk.
4 I need some paper to write on.
5 They seemed to have already left.

unit 03 부사적 용법
p.83

EXERCISES

A

1 to play 　　　　 2 meet
3 to go 　　　　　 4 enough to follow
5 check 　　　　　 6 get
7 to relieve

B

1 F, went → to go
2 T
3 F, saw → to see
4 F, borrows → to borrow
5 T
6 F, bought → to buy
7 F, misses → to miss

C

⑤ to killing → to kill

Workbook

A

1 get 　　　 2 accept 　　　 3 win
4 learn 　　 5 see

B

①, ③, ④

C

1 We went to the airport to
2 She grew up to be a great scientist.
3 We were happy to see him alive.
4 She was wise to stay at home.
5 We went to Canada to learn English.

unit 04 to 부정사 관용 표현
p.85

EXERCISES

A

1 too shy 　　　　　 2 too young
3 foolish enough 　　 4 in order to relax
5 so as to see 　　　 6 to leave
7 to dump

B

1 F, enough brave → brave enough
2 F, good too → too good
3 F, in to order → in order to
4 T
5 F, but sell → but to sell
6 F, believe → to believe
7 T

C

③ In order do this → In order to do this

Workbook

A

1 understand 　　 2 refuse
3 build 　　　　　 4 leave
5 begin

B

①, ③, ④

C

1 He is too young to ride a horse.
2 She was so kind as to guide me.
3 In order to live happily
4 I had no choice but to sell the computer.
5 To be frank with you, I love Erica.

p.87

EXERCISES

A

1 happen	2 understood	3 injured
4 played	5 kick	6 move
7 read		

B

1 T

2 F, studied → study

3 F, to cut → cut

4 F, call → called

5 F, beaten → beat [beating]

6 F, to wait → wait

7 T

C

⑤ became → become

Workbook

A

| 1 taken | 2 play | 3 laughing |
| 4 weep | 5 drive | |

B

①, ④, ⑤

C

1 He saw someone break into his house.

2 She had her computer repaired.

3 We saw Mary play the piano.

4 We did nothing but eat and sleep.

5 He had his wallet stolen.

Chapter Review

A

1 moving → to move
* want는 to부정사를 목적어로 취하는 동사이다.

2 bought → to buy
* decide는 to부정사를 목적어로 취하는 동사이다.

3 help → to help
* refuse는 to부정사를 목적어로 취하는 동사이다.

4 meeting → to meet
* expect는 to부정사를 목적어로 취하는 동사이다.

5 built → to build
* hope은 to부정사를 목적어로 취하는 동사이다.

6 clean → to clean
* broom을 꾸며주는 형용사적 용법의 to부정사를 써야 한다.

7 helped → to help
* assistant를 꾸며주는 형용사적 용법의 to부정사를 써야 한다.

8 were → be
* seem 다음에 to부정사가 와야 한다.

9 love → to love
* come 다음에 to부정사가 와야 한다.

10 hold → held
* 수동의 의미이기 때문에 be 다음에 과거분사가 와야 한다.

11 caught → to catch
* 목적을 나타내는 부사적 용법의 to부정사를 써야 한다.

12 hearing → hear
* 감정의 원인을 나타내는 부사적 용법의 to부정사를 써야 한다.

13 be → to be
* 결과를 나타내는 부사적 용법의 to부정사를 써야 한다.

14 got → get
* 목적을 나타내는 부사적 용법의 to부정사를 써야 한다.

15 met → to meet
* 목적을 나타내는 부사적 용법의 to부정사를 써야 한다.

16 careless too → too careless
* "too ~ to …"라는 형식이므로 careless가 too 다음에 와야 한다.

17 enough wise → wise enough
- enough은 형용사를 꾸미는 경우에 형용사 다음에 와야 한다.

18 solved → solve
- "too ~ to …"라는 형식이므로 to부정사 형태로 써야 한다.

19 In to order → In order to
- "~하기 위해서"는 "in order to ~"라는 형식으로 써야 한다.

20 move → to move
- "have no choice but to ~"라는 형식으로 써야 한다.

21 cleans → cleaned
- 수동의 관계이기 때문에 목적격보어로 과거분사를 써야 한다.

22 worked → work
- 능동의 관계이기 때문에 목적격보어로 원형부정사를 써야 한다.

23 massage → massaged
- 수동의 관계이기 때문에 목적격보어로 과거분사를 써야 한다.

24 selling → sell
- "would rather 원형부정사 than 원형부정사"의 형식으로 써야 한다.

25 to sing → sing
- "do nothing but 원형부정사"라는 형식으로 써야 한다.

B
④

C
② written → to write

D
1 c	2 d	3 b
4 a	5 c	6 b
7 a	8 b	9 d
10 a	11 b	12 c
13 d	14 b	15 c
16 d	17 b	18 c
19 d	20 b	

---

unit 01 동명사의 형태와 쓰임새
p.95

EXERCISES

A
1 Watching	2 writing	3 living
4 build	5 used	6 driving
7 practicing		

B
1 T
2 F, to work → working
3 F, was used → used
4 T
5 F, to live → to living
6 F, relaxed → relaxing [to relax]
7 F, to watch → watching

C
③ to go → going

Workbook

A
1 Growing	2 taking
3 reading	4 using
5 eating	

B
②, ③, ④, ⑤

C
1 finished our homework yet
2 hate working at the office on Mondays
3 not interested in studying abroad
4 more fun than playing tennis
5 Mastering a foreign language

EXERCISES

A

1 Swimming 2 having
3 having 4 having
5 having 6 having been
7 having

B

1 T
2 F, being → having
3 F, being → having
4 F
5 F, being interviewed → having interviewed
6 T
7 F, being cheated → having cheated

C

④ Being thought → Thinking

Workbook

A

1 having cheated
2 completing [having completed]
3 being scolded
4 being served
5 doing

B

①, ②, ⑤

C

1 hated being called sweetie
2 having met me before
3 the party without being invited
4 having traveled in Europe for a month
5 admitted having made a mistake

EXERCISES

A

1 having 2 writing 3 to sell
4 watching 5 breathing
6 having 7 helping

B

1 T
2 F, building → to build
3 F, telling → to tell
4 F, staying → to stay
5 F, to have → having
6 F, to have → having
7 F, to have → having

C

⑤ to eat → eating

Workbook

A

1 closing 2 to bring
3 to buy 4 to play
5 having

B

①, ③, ⑤

C

1 He forgot to bring his passport.
2 We enjoyed swimming in the lake.
3 She finished writing her report.
4 We decided to master English.
5 We want to build a better world.

EXERCISES

A

1	telling	2	reading
3	drinking	4	meeting
5	had	6	began
7	to see		

B

1 T
2 F, he had → had he
3 F, she had → had she
4 T
5 F, of to go → of going
6 F, attacked → attacking
7 F, to explore → exploring

C

⑤ to regain → regaining

Workbook

A

1	telling	2	reading
3	watching	4	treating
5	visiting		

B

①, ④, ⑤

C

1 It's no use advising him.
2 Her poem is worth reading.
3 I feel like seeing a play today.
4 On seeing him, she burst into tears.
5 He was on the point of opening the door.

Chapter Review

A

1 Drink → Drinking
  • 주어 역할을 맡을 수 있는 동명사를 써야 한다.

2 driven → driving
  • "~하는 데 익숙하다"는 뜻으로 to 다음에 동명사를 써야 한다.

3 making → make
  • "~하기 위해 사용되다"는 뜻으로 to 다음에 동사원형이 와야 한다.

4 were used → used
  • "~였다"는 뜻이기 때문에 used to를 써야 한다.

5 to relax → relaxing
  • 전치사의 목적어이므로 반드시 동명사를 써야 한다.

6 to make → making
  • "spend+시간+동명사" 형식으로 써야 한다.

7 play → playing
  • 전치사의 목적어이므로 반드시 동명사를 써야 한다.

8 being → having
  • 능동의 개념이기 때문에 being을 쓸 수 없다.

9 having been → having
  • 능동의 개념이기 때문에 been을 쓸 수 없다.

10 being → having
  • 능동의 개념이기 때문에 being을 쓸 수 없다.

11 having being → having
  • 능동의 개념이기 때문에 being을 쓸 수 없다.

12 having → being
  • 수동의 개념이기 때문에 being을 써야 한다.

13 being → having
  • 능동의 개념이기 때문에 being을 쓸 수 없다.

14 to listen → listening
  • enjoy는 동명사만을 목적어로 취하는 동사이다.

15 to help → helping
  • mind는 동명사만을 목적어로 취하는 동사이다.

16 to write → writing
  • finish는 동명사만을 목적어로 취하는 동사이다.

17 to make → making
  • 과거에 대한 내용이기 때문에 동명사가 와야 한다.

18 taking → to take
  • "휴식을 취하기 위해서"이기 때문에 to부정사를 써야 한다.

19 becoming → to become
  • want는 to부정사를 목적어로 취하는 대표적인 동사이다.

20 living → to live

  • choose는 to부정사를 목적어로 취하는 대표적인 동사이다.

21 tell → telling

  • 동명사의 관용 표현으로 반드시 -ing형을 써야 한다.

22 watching them → watching

  • 주어인 The film *E.T.*가 watch의 목적어 역할을 하므로 반복해서 나타내지 않는다.

23 to drink → drinking

  • 전치사의 목적어이므로 반드시 동명사를 사용해야 한다.

24 he had → had he

  • 부정어가 문두에 오면 주어와 동사가 도치된다.

25 to do → doing

  • 전치사의 목적어이므로 반드시 동명사를 사용해야 한다.

B

④

C

③ to help → helping

D

1 d	2 c	3 d
4 b	5 c	6 d
7 b	8 c	9 b
10 c	11 d	12 c
13 b	14 c	15 b
16 d	17 b	18 c
19 d	20 b	

Chapter 7 _ 분사

unit 01 분사의 형태와 쓰임새
p.109

EXERCISES

A

1	watching	2	sleeping
3	eaten	4	awakened
5	talking	6	required
7	falling snow		

B

1 T
2 F, watching → watched
3 F, talked → talking
4 T
5 F, cooked → cooking
6 T
7 F, Run → Running

C

⑤ unanswering → unanswered

Workbook

A

1	shocking	2	confusing
3	rolling	4	directed
5	surprised		

B

③, ④, ⑤

C

1 is cleaning the room right now
2 sleeping dog was awakened
3 smelled burnt cake in the oven
4 fill in the required document
5 falling snow covered everything

unit 02 현재분사 vs. 동명사

p.111

EXERCISES

A

1 분   2 분   3 동   4 분

5 분   6 동   7 동

B

1 F, plays → playing

2 T

3 F, Play → Playing

4 F, watched → watching

5 T

6 F, seeing → seen

7 F, We reading → We are reading

C

③ to work → working

Workbook

A

1 studying   2 singing

3 reading   4 fishing

5 writing

B

③, ④, ⑤

C

1 Eating breakfast is good

2 is learning how to do gymnastics

3 went swimming in the lake

4 I was unlocking the door.

5 The movie was very moving.

unit 03 현재분사 vs. 과거분사

p.113

EXERCISES

A

1 talked   2 complaining

3 used   4 barking

5 broken   6 standing

7 stealing

B

1 F, gone → going

2 F, exciting → excited

3 F, wrapping → wrapped

4 F, shocking → shocked

5 T

6 F, watched → watching

7 T

C

② detailing → detailed

Workbook

A

1 interested   2 named

3 amazing   4 screaming

5 threatening

B

②, ③, ⑤

C

1 is watering the flower garden

2 looked puzzled at the news

3 is a very boring person

4 Her new album released last week

5 eating pizza at the new restaurant

unit 04 분사구문의 형태와 쓰임새
p.115

EXERCISES

A

1 While   2 As   3 Because
4 While

B

1 Taking off his jacket
2 Not having finished it
3 Being so scared
4 Checking his email

C

② played → playing

Workbook

A

1 Raised [Having been raised]
2 working
3 Not knowing
4 Being
5 Satisfied

B

②, ③, ⑤

C

1 having no money
2 Learning to play the piano
3 Taking off his jacket
4 Speaking to the whole class
5 Rescued from the tree

Chapter Review

A

1 wore → wearing
  * 능동의 의미를 나타내기 때문에 현재분사를 써야
    한다.

2 surprising → surprised
  * 수동의 의미를 나타내기 때문에 과거분사를 써야
    한다.

3 bored → boring
  * 감정을 유발하는 것이기 때문에 현재분사를 써야
    한다.

4 excited → exciting
  * 감정을 유발하는 것이기 때문에 현재분사를 써야
    한다.

5 played → playing
  * 현재완료진행형으로 현재분사를 써야 한다.

6 burning → burned [burnt]
  * 수동의 관계이기 때문에 과거분사를 써야 한다.

7 played → playing
  * 현재진행형으로 현재분사를 써야 한다.

8 writing → written
  * 수동태이기 때문에 과거분사를 써야 한다.

9 painting → painted
  * 수동의 관계이기 때문에 과거분사를 써야 한다.

10 worrying → worried
  * 감정을 느끼는 것이기 때문에 과거분사를 써야
    한다.

11 disappointed → disappointing
  * 감정을 유발하는 것이기 때문에 현재분사를 써야
    한다.

12 desk broken → broken desk
  * 명사를 홀로 수식하는 경우 과거분사는 명사 앞에
    놓여야 한다.

13 interested → interesting
  * 감정을 유발하는 것이기 때문에 현재분사를 써야
    한다.

14 lived → living
  * 진행의 의미를 나타내기 때문에 현재분사를 써야
    한다.

15 being → been
  * 현재완료형이기 때문에 과거분사를 써야 한다.

16 satisfying → satisfied
  * 감정을 느끼는 것이기 때문에 과거분사를 써야
    한다.

17 read → reading
  * 현재신행형으로 현새분사를 써야 한다.

18 looked → looking
   * 능동의 의미를 나타내기 때문에 현재분사를 써야
     한다.

19 amazed → amazing
   * 감정을 유발하는 것이기 때문에 현재분사를 써야
     한다.

20 stolen → stealing
   * 능동의 의미를 나타내기 때문에 현재분사를 써야
     한다.

21 Walk → Walking
   * 분사구문이기 때문에 현재분사로 시작해야 한다.

22 Seen → Seeing
   * 분사구문이기 때문에 현재분사로 시작해야 한다.

23 She losing → Losing
   * 분사구문의 주어가 주절의 주어와 일치하므로
     생략해야 한다.

24 If finding → Finding [Having found]
   * 조건의 의미가 아니므로 If를 쓸 이유가 없다.

25 Knowing not → Not knowing
   * 분사구문의 부정은 부정어를 분사 앞에 붙여야
     한다.

B
③

C
② impressing → impressed

D

1 c	2 c	3 c
4 b	5 c	6 c
7 c	8 d	9 b
10 b	11 b	12 c
13 a	14 b	15 c
16 a	17 c	18 c
19 c	20 b	

Chapter 8 _ 가정법

unit 01 가정법의 형태와 쓰임새
p.123

EXERCISES

A

1 were		2 were		3 had	
4 had		5 leave		6 go	
7 wait					

B
1 T
2 F, have seen → had seen
3 T
4 F, sent → send
5 F, was → be
6 T
7 F, had told → tell

C
② sent → send

Workbook
A

1 were	2 participate
3 took	4 had known
5 had	

B
①, ③, ④

C

1 I would not read such a book
2 you would not have made such a
  mistake
3 would not have waited so long

EXERCISES

A

1 were   2 could   3 were
4 played   5 drove   6 were to
7 didn't

B

1 F, bought → would buy
2 F, wasn't → didn't
3 F, join → joined
4 F, will buy → would buy
5 F, will → would
6 F, am → were
7 F, will → would

C

⑤ to develop → developed

Workbook

A

1 had   2 were   3 joined
4 go   5 take

B

②, ③, ⑤

C

1 the weather were fine, we would go fishing
2 there were a vending machine in the office, that would help us
3 she were not a vegetarian, I would go to the restaurant with her.

EXERCISES

A

1 had practiced   2 had asked
3 had woken up   4 hadn't driven
5 would have loved 6 have
7 Had

B

1 F, had helped → helped
2 F, went → had gone
3 F, have been → had been
4 T
5 T
6 T
7 F, could open → could have opened

C

③ had → have

Workbook

A

1 had not gone
2 would not have been
3 would have met
4 had studied
5 had not been

B

②, ④, ⑤

C

1 she had lost her wallet, she would have cried
2 you had not eaten so much, you would not have been sick
3 I had worked harder, I would have made more money.

EXERCISES

A

1 were	2 had gone
3 had bought	4 had been
5 had visited	6 went
7 had	

B

1 F, haven't said → hadn't said
2 T
3 T
4 F, have → had
5 F, will be → were
6 F, knows → knew
7 T

C

② will → would

Workbook

A

1 were	2 had gotten	3 had written

B

②, ③

C

1 wish I had a dog
2 wish I spoke Japanese well
3 as if she were a millionaire
4 acts as if he were my boyfriend
5 speaks as if she were an expert

Chapter Review

A

1 went → go
   · 요구를 나타내는 ask 다음의 that절에서는 동사원형을 써야 한다.
2 will watch → watch
   · 제안을 나타내는 suggest 다음의 that절에서는 동사원형을 써야 한다.
3 called → call
   · 요구를 나타내는 demand 다음의 that절에서는 동사원형을 써야 한다.
4 passed → pass
   · 제안을 나타내는 propose 다음의 that절에서는 동사원형을 써야 한다.
5 are → be
   · 명령을 나타내는 order 다음의 that절에서는 동사원형을 써야 한다.
6 study → studied
   · 가정법 과거이므로 if절에는 동사의 과거형을 써야 한다.
7 was → were
   · 가정법 과거이므로 if절에는 were를 써야 한다.
8 will → would
   · 가정법 과거이므로 귀결절에서는 조동사의 과거형을 써야 한다.
9 am → were
   · 가정법 과거이므로 if절에는 were를 써야 한다.
10 can → could
   · 가정법 과거이므로 귀결절에서는 조동사의 과거형을 써야 한다.
11 ate → eaten
   · 가정법 과거완료이므로 if절에서는 "had 과거분사"를 써야 한다.
12 brought → had brought
   · 가정법 과거완료이므로 if절에서는 "had 과거분사"를 써야 한다.
13 will → would
   · 가정법 과거완료이므로 귀결절에서는 조동사의 과거형을 써야 한다.
14 did → had
   · 가정법 과거완료이므로 if절에서는 "had 과거분사"를 써야 한다.
15 went → had gone
   · 가정법 과거완료이므로 if절에서는 "had 과거분사"를 써야 한다.

16 had brought → had not brought or
would have → would not have
* 내용으로 보아 if절이나 귀결절의 내용이 부정이어
야 한다.

17 would help → would have helped
* 가정법 과거완료이므로 귀결절은 "would +
have + 과거분사"여야 한다.

18 didn't spend → hadn't spent
* 과거에 대한 내용이므로 가정법 과거완료로 표현
해야 한다.

19 was → were
* 가정법 과거이므로 if절에는 were를 써야 한다.

20 will → would
* 가정법 과거이므로 귀결절에서는 조동사의 과거형
을 써야 한다.

21 start → started
* "It's about time + 주어 + 가정법 과거" 형식으로
써야 한다.

22 was → were
* 가정법 과거이므로 be동사는 반드시 were를
써야 한다.

23 will be → were
* 가정법 과거 형식이므로 be동사는 반드시 were를
써야 한다.

24 would watch → would have watched
* 가정법 과거완료이므로 귀결절은 "would +
have + 과거분사"여야 한다.

25 left → had left
* 가정법 과거완료이므로 if절에서는 "had 과거분사"
를 써야 한다.

B
③

C
④ have → had

D

1 c	2 b	3 b
4 d	5 d	6 a
7 b	8 c	9 d
10 b	11 b	12 d
13 d	14 b	15 b
16 c	17 c	18 c
19 d	20 c	

Chapter 9 _ 일치와 화법

unit 01 수의 일치
p.137

EXERCISES

A

1 play	2 are
3 are	4 is
5 understands	6 are
7 are	

B

1 F, are → is
2 T
3 T
4 T
5 F, is → are
6 F, are → is
7 T

C
⑤ want → wants

Workbook

A

1 like	2 is	3 is
4 wants	5 run	

B
③, ④

C

1 One of us has to look after
2 Either you or he has to
3 Both he and his wife want to adopt a
child.

unit 02 시제 일치
p.139

EXERCISES

A

1 was   2 had drunk   3 would
4 would   5 took
6 broke   7 was

B

1 T
2 F, will go → would go
3 F, will be → would be
4 T
5 F, lies → lied
6 F, am → was
7 T

C

② will → would

Workbook

A

1 is   2 fell   3 majored
4 was   5 built

B

①, ③, ④

C

1 We believed that you did your best.
2 French is an official language of Canada
3 Our science teacher said that water consists of oxygen and hydrogen.

unit 03 화법의 종류와 쓰임새
p.141

EXERCISES

A

1 the following day   2 said
3 said   4 is
5 tomorrow   6 was

B

1 F, She said that she had been sick the previous day.
2 F, Sammy says that she is hungry.
3 F, Bob told us that we had to finish that in an hour.
4 T
5 F, He said that they were getting married there.

C

⑤ want → wanted

Workbook

A

1 would see   2 had lived   3 told

B

②, ④, ⑤

C

1 She told me that she had a great plan.
2 She says that her hobby used to be collecting stamps.
3 Adams said that the earth moves around the sun.

EXERCISES

A

1 asked   2 if   3 if
4 wanted   5 she kept

B

1 T
2 F, She asked me where I lived.
3 F, He asked me if I liked reading comic books.
4 F, My friend asked me why I was so angry.
5 F, She asked him whether he spoke Spanish.

C

① what is my wish → what my wish is

Workbook

A

1 had suffered   2 had lied
3 had solved   4 wanted
5 had come

B

①, ④, ⑤

C

1 The teacher asked us if we understood what he said.
2 He asked me how long I would stay in Spain.
3 She asked me if I could lend her money.

EXERCISES

A

1 told   2 to take   3 her
4 going   5 not to run

B

1 F, He asked me to bring him some food.
2 T
3 F, I advised him to go home before dark.
4 F, Dad warned me not to bother him.
5 T

C

⑤ to not look into it → not to look into it

Workbook

A

1 not to forget   2 go
3 to take

B

②, ③

C

1 My boss warned me not to be late again.
2 My coach advised me to lose weight.
3 My boyfriend suggested that we go to a concert.

Chapter Review

A

1 am → are
   * and로 이어져서 복수 개념을 나타내므로 동사는 복수형을 써야 한다.

2 have → has
   * either A or B는 B에 수를 일치시킨다.

3 have → has
   * each나 every 다음에 and로 연결된 주어가 오더라도 동사는 단수형을 취한다.

4 are → is
   * not only A but also B → B에 수를 일치시킨다.

5 was → were
   * and로 이어져서 복수 개념을 나타내므로 동사는 복수형을 써야 한다.

6 is → are
   * of 다음에 복수가 왔기 때문에 동사도 복수형을 써야 한다.

7 were → was
   * Romeo and Juliet 전체가 하나의 작품을 나타내기 때문에 단수형을 써야 한다.

8 were → was
   * of 다음에 불가산명사가 왔기 때문에 동사는 단수형을 써야 한다.

9 will → would
   * 시제 일치에 따라 과거형 다음에는 과거 또는 과거완료가 와야 한다.

10 have → had, yesterday → the previous day
   * 시제 일치에 따라 과거형 다음에 과거완료를 써야 하고 부사 표현을 알맞게 고친다.

11 is → are
   * 주어가 CDs로 복수형이기 때문에 동사는 복수형을 써야 한다.

12 went → goes
   * 현재의 습관을 나타내기 때문에 현재시제를 써야 한다.

13 told → said
   * 직접화법에 알맞은 전달동사는 said이다.

14 wants → wanted
   * 시제 일치에 따라 과거형 다음에는 과거 또는 과거완료가 와야 한다.

15 will → would
   * 시제 일치에 따라 과거형 다음에는 과거 또는 과거완료가 와야 한다.

16 will live → lived
   * 과거 시점에서 말하고 있으므로 동사는 과거시제를 써야 한다.

17 was → were
   * of 다음에 복수가 왔기 때문에 동사도 복수형을 써야 한다.

18 are → is
   * 주어가 one으로 단수이기 때문에 동사도 단수형을 써야 한다.

19 knows → knew
   * 시제 일치에 따라 과거형 다음에는 과거 또는 과거완료가 와야 한다.

20 A stranger asked me if I could tell him [her] where the nearest bank was.
   * 상황에 맞게 간접화법으로 옮겨야 한다.

21 how was my day → how my day was
   * 간접의문문이기 때문에 "의문사+주어+동사"라는 어순이 되어야 한다.

22 looks → looked
   * 시제 일치에 따라 과거형 다음에는 과거 또는 과거완료가 와야 한다.

23 says → asked
   * 맥락으로 보아 간접화법을 써야 하므로 전달동사는 asked를 사용해야 한다.

24 me → her
   * 인칭대명사는 상황에 맞게 바꾸어야 한다.

25 help → to help
   * 명령문의 화법 전환으로 asked의 목적격보어로 to부정사가 와야 한다.

B

④

C

③ to see not → not to see

D

1 c	2 a	3 a
4 b	5 c	6 d
7 d	8 a	9 c
10 b	11 b	12 d
13 c	14 b	15 b
16 a	17 b	18 a
19 c	20 c	

TOP GRAMMAR

For Intermediate Students - 1

정답 및 해설